The Norfolk Connection

Keith Skipper

This is the place: stand still my steed,
Let me review the scene
And summon from the shadowy past
The forms that once have been.
(From "A Gleam of Sunlight" by Longfellow)

Poppyland Publishing

© 1991 Keith Skipper
Printed by Printing Services (Norwich) Ltd
Front cover design by Top Floor Design
First published 1991 by Poppyland Publishing
ISBN 0 946148 48 1

Foreword

Charles Roberts, Arts Editor, Eastern Daily Press

There was a time, only a very few years ago, when Norfolk effortlessly absorbed its newcomers, converting them so subtly, so quietly, to its own gentle rhythms - and instilling into them an instinctive appreciation of its age-old, distinctive personality.

Has old Norfolk of late been too sure, too confident, of its enduring individuality? Because something is going wrong, the old certainties, the old continuities, are in danger. There's a new breed at large, here as elsewhere, upon whom the influence of tradition and history, of the native vernacular of a place, is as impervious as water on an otter's pelt.

To such their brash credo is simply: Think not what Norfolk wants - But seek to impose upon it that which you think it ought to have.

Recently, at long last, a highly-placed 'local' voice spoke out, when the High Sheriff attacked the greed and insensitivity of developers who already are raping this county for their short-term gain. It was headline news! Yet others have been voicing the same warnings, and more, for some years past. Not least among them has been Keith Skipper who has, with unfailing good humour (spiked occasionally with a mite of vitriol) become through Radio Norfolk a doughty banner bearer in defence of this county and its spirit.

I can't claim to be a native like him. But, 23 years on, I think I'm firmly adopted. This is an area - idiosyncrasies, flaws and all - which I quickly came to love and, as is often the case with converts, became as passionate in the faith (and probably more so) as any local. Just as Keith Skipper has employed the air waves, so it has been my aim to speak through the Eastern Daily Press in praise and defence and encouragement of that which is good and sound and worthy of cherishing under our broad Norfolk sky.

If such resolution needs stiffening, one has only to read Keith's latest opus to be reminded in what splendid footsteps we march. Members of the great mardling club in the sky all the worthies galleried may be: but what resonant echoes of words, character and example they have left behind to inspire us.

I knew but a handful of them - Aubrey Aitken, beloved Bishop of Lynn, who used his gravelled voice of later years with a drama to excite and to make vivid the simplest message; Dick Bagnall-Oakeley, through whom I first encountered the sheer delight of laid-back Norfolk humour...

Ted Ellis, enchantingly gentle and warm, with the mien of an absent-minded professor and the natural history knowledge of a whole shelf of encyclopaedias; Bishop Launcelot Fleming, a patrician of the old school yet with the steel and resolution to carry through reforms which earned him as much opprobrium as appreciation...

Eric Fowler, fondly remembered EDP colleague, essayist in the great tradition of Hazlitt, and unfailingly kind and thoughtful soul; and Sir Lincoln Ralphs, who as Norfolk's education supremo towered over the county in his unforgettable dynamism and personality.

Yet Keith Skipper - who here underlines, if one needed to be told, how literary and scholarly he is under that bluff-bearded, punning exterior - has taken us back through the millennia to focus our attention on other great names, introducing us en route to quite a few we'd never heard of.

Sarah Glover, inventor of tonic sol fa, was new to me. As was the 18th century squire Robert Marsham, to whom I warmed at once, for he spent his life planting trees...What a wonderful way to be remembered. Truly he left his mark, graphically, on his corner of Norfolk. As, in their different ways, did all those gathered in these pages.

Few of us may aspire to the achievements of these worthy folk. But just by standing up and speaking out for Norfolk now, when she needs help most, we can in some small measure contribute to the great stream of which they are a part.

C V R
Saxham
July 1991

Acknowledgements

The value of my own Norfolk connections has been underlined many times in compiling this volume, and I am deeply grateful to all who have gone out of their way to help.

I consulted hundreds of local books and magazines, giving regular thanks for the rich fund of information available, but I also owe a big debt to many people who share with me a deep pride in the old county.

Details and photographs came from various quarters, and I thank all who assisted with these. Even so, extra salutes are in order after an invigorating whistle-stop tour through Norfolk history to find numerous examples of present-day co-operation.

My special thanks to: David Newham, who spearheaded regular raids on the Eastern Counties Newspapers files for both articles and pictures; Chris Weston, a fellow-traveller on the Sheringham-Norwich railway line and such a cheerful ally in making tracks to far-flung research departments; Brian Hedge for his customary unflappable assistance with illustrations; Peter and Brenda Stibbons, of Poppyland Publishing, for their enthusiastic backing of this project from the start; Charles Roberts, one of the area's busiest and most talented artistic all-rounders, for his typically erudite and supportive foreword.

Smiles of appreciation also for: Meg Aitken, Jeremy Bagnall-Oakeley, Bob Bagshaw, Jim Baldwin, John Baxter, David Butters, Lorna Clarke, Terry Davy, Alwyn Edgar, Noel Edwards, Dick Futter, Ted Goodwyn, Alan Howard, Cyril Jolly, Sir Julian Paget, Michale Seago, Edward Skipper, David Turner, Carol Twinch, David Wakefield and Great Yarmouth Central Library.

To all other individuals and organisations who helped, my thanks.

Finally, a song of praise for my wife, Diane. She confronted the word processor with confidence and industry after I had confined my technological talents to the steam-driven typewriter up the corner.

Keith Skipper
Cromer 1991

Introduction

The spur for this book was a night of blank faces at Sheringham's Little Theatre.

I was guest questionmaster for the final of the town quiz, and the bonus was to be asked to set a round of my own choice. I posed six questions with a local flavour. They all but drew a blank, in marked contrast to most of the other two dozen rounds as the finalists made short work of mathematics, geography, science, classical music...

Mystified looks and eerie silences greeted my round - and I didn't think questions about the birthplace of farmworkers' leader George Edwards or the identity of the Norfolk humourist born at Potter Heigham in 1888 were all that difficult.

I expressed my surprise and disappointment in an article in the Eastern Daily Press soon after, suggesting little attention was paid in our schools to outstanding local characters. My remarks prompted some lively correspondence to the paper, one letter pointing out that as a journalist I had the time, inclination and opportunity to follow up obscure knowledge. "Like all people who have an interest in the subject, he thinks it should be common knowledge to all."

Well, I could not accept that being interested in people with Norfolk connections, many of them quite famous beyond the county boundaries, should be regarded as pursuing the obscure, and I continue to feel strongly that their exploits should be recognised by many more people, especially those who live in Norfolk today.

To this end, I started collating characters worthy of a place in a lengthy cavalcade, and it staggered me to find I had almost reached the hundred without diversions towards any unlikely areas.

All characters in this Norfolk "hall of fame" are members of the Great Mardling Club in the Sky - the only definite stipulation I made. It is by no means an exhaustive list, and it reflects my own interests to some degree. But I did try to renew acquaintance with as wide a cross-section as possible - including several personalities who made a mark in more recent times. I knew most of them.

Many of the characters on my list were born in Norfolk, and moved on to find fame - like Horatio Nelson, Astley Cooper, Jem Mace, Thomas Paine and Edith Cavell.

Some spent their twilight years in the county or had established a strong reputation before moving here - for example William Cowper, Henry Williamson and Frederick Marryatt.

Many simply dominated the Norfolk stage, or their particular part of it, for much of their lives - Henry Blogg, Ted Ellis, Jeremiah Colman, George Edwards - while some take their places as a result of finding fresh impetus on visiting the old county. Clement Scott, the man who fell in love with "Poppyland", and Jenny Lind, the Swedish Nightingale who founded the children's hospital in Norwich, stand out in this section.

Of course, many personalities were automatic selections, having already demanded chapters in the national and international history books - Boadicea, John Fastolf, Henry Rider Haggard, Robert Kett, Lord Nelson and Anne Boleyn among them. Quite a few have been the subject of a book on their own.

These thumbnail sketches will act, I hope, as a little inducement to move on, to find out more as you haunt the bookshelves for even wider Norfolk connections.

Some names may not be too familiar, but they fully deserve spots on the podium. There's Thomas Baines, the news artist; William D'Oyley, the road safety pioneer; Nathaniel Gill, the defiant preacher; William Crotch, the musical whizz-kid.

As it was impossible to mention one without the other, I decided to include Tom and Kitty Higdon, the Burston School strike teachers, as a single entry. Another family link concerns Howard Carter, the Swaffham man who uncovered Tutankhamun's tomb, and Harry Carter, whose wonderful town and village signs are dotted across Norfolk. They were cousins - and Harry Carter would have been entitled to his place even if he hadn't been my art and woodwork teacher at Hamond's Grammar School in Swaffham!

Religious figures do well on this roll of honour, and James Woodforde and Benjamin Armstrong must have known even while they were penning those famous diaries that such industry could well be rewarded a few years later in a volume such as this. More contemporary church figures like Aubrey Aitken, Noel Boston and Launcelot Fleming were easy to include when it came to taking up the modern collection.

For a few, perhaps, a salute here might bring more praise and recognition, albeit rather belatedly.

Mary Mann's Norfolk stories, first published at the turn of the century, dealt with stark rural deprivation rather than the more marketable rustic charm. These harrowing tales not only put the 'good old days' into perspective, but emphasise the qualities of a local writer who has been sadly neglected.

Howard Carter's amazing discoveries in Egypt, and the dedicated work he carried out in the years before Tutankhamun's tomb came to light, have never been fully appreciated in his native county in general or in his home town of Swaffham in particular.

Sarah Martin, of Caister-on-Sea, is an unsung heroine. While Elizabeth Fry's work in the field of prison reform is well chronicled and rightly lauded, Sarah Martin's efforts in the same area have been ignored all too often.

In any event, here are well over 100 characters with the special Norfolk connection. As you make comparisons, and push forward candidates of your own, try this little exercise...

With which three people featured in this book would you most like to share a dinner party - a meal and a mardle?

After a lot of deliberation I have settled for Mary Mann, Jem Mace and Howard Carter. Writer, fighter and treasure-seeker.

Any chance of Benjamin Armstrong dropping in to say grace? Perhaps Jenny Lind and Sidney Grapes would sort out some after-dinner entertainment? What about Will Kemp and Nugent Monck taking us on to a show? Boadicea to provide transport and William Faden the map?

That's the trouble with the Norfolk connection. Once you have made it, you don't know where to stop.

Keith Skipper

James Adams (1839-1903)

Clergyman hero

The first clergyman to be awarded the Victoria Cross, James Adam settled in Norfolk, first in Postwick, near Norwich, and then moved on to Stow Bardolph in the Fens. He won the VC during the Afghan War. He went to the aid of a wounded lancer and then, still under "an accurate and galling fire", he rescued two more men trapped beneath their horses. He hauled the two cavalrymen from under their mounts in the ditch while the water around him foamed with crashing hooves and flying bullets.

When the fighting ended Lord Roberts, Victorian England's most popular soldier hero - who had seen the courageous Adams in action - recommended him for the VC, the nation's highest award for martial valour. In fact, as a civilian clergyman, Adams was ineligible for the medal, but under pressure from Roberts the rules were altered to allow the padre to become the first man of the cloth to win the VC.

In India James William Adams worked gallantly in the smallpox camps, attributing his escape from the disease to seven yearly inoculations, and a glass of sherry each time he entered the camp.

He held the living at Postwick from 1887 to 1894 and then moved to Stow Bardolph, where his flock was scattered among the Fenland farming families. For those who could not reach the church at Stow Bardolph or Wimbotsham, he held a special afternoon service in a schoolroom hired at Stow Bridge. There he would set up his wooden table and preach, as he had done to the soldiers in Afghanistan. He died in 1903, only a year after leaving his Fenland parish.

When, after his death, Stow Mission was built, his widow gave to it the portable altar and communion table he had used in battle as sole civilian chaplain accompanying the powerful British army of invasion.

Aubrey Aitken (1912-1985)

Sporting Bishop

One of Norfolk's best-loved characters of recent times, Aubrey Aitken, the Bishop of Lynn, died at 73. Born in North Walsham he had been Bishop of Lynn for a dozen years and, before that, Archdeacon of Norwich for a similar period. A keen all-round sportsman he played cricket and rugby in his early days.

Only a few months before his death he conducted a service to mark the centenary of Norwich Rugby Club - an event thought to be unique in sporting history. He was a former president of the rugby club, but it was his love of Norwich City Football Club that enhanced his sporting reputation.

He was made an honorary life vice-president of the Canaries in 1979, the first time the board had gone outside Carrow Road to make such an appointment. His last sermon, three weeks before he died, was in the Hempnall group of parishes; the congregation gave him three cheers!

The Eastern Daily Press, to which he was a regular contributor, paid this tribute: "As a Bishop, Aubrey Aitken would have been a conspicuous figure even in an age less grey and of more robust spiritual certitude than the present. He embodied much that is best and most attractive in the Anglican tradition; a direct faith, breadth of sympathy, companionable instincts and a deep attachment to his native land and its people. Here was a good man who believed that it was better to light a candle than to curse the darkness."

He had part of his vocal cords removed, but carried on preaching with the aid of a microphone - something he didn't need to play a full part in after-match discussions

at Carrow Road. He saw his first football match on November 29th 1919, when Norwich City defeated Gillingham 5-0 in the Southern League. "My only memory of that game is of the tall Gillingham goalkeeper, who wore a long, white cricket sweater, turning unhappily to pick the ball out of the net five times. My young heart bled for him. But as the years have gone by I have become less sympathetic towards opposing goalkeepers" he wrote in 1976 in his introduction to "On The Ball, City", a history of his beloved Norwich City by Ted Bell.

Benjamin Armstrong (1817-1890)

Dereham diaries

Vicar of East Dereham from 1850 until 1888, Armstrong's Norfolk diaries covering those years reveal a highly intelligent, educated and observant country parson. He graduated from Cambridge, was ordained a deacon in 1841 and a priest the following year. After holding two curacies he became incumbent of Little Stanmore in Middlesex, before moving to the considerable Norfolk parish of Dereham. He is buried in Dereham churchyard.

The first volume of extracts from his diaries was published in 1949 and in his foreword his grandson, the Rev Herbert B J Armstrong of King's Lynn, wrote: "His theological outlook was that of an old-fashioned Tractarian, and he was regarded by the then Diocesan authorities as being a dangerous man in consequence. His love for his people and his diligence in ministries to them was never denied."

Benjamin John Armstrong was knowledgeable about farming and country affairs. He could derive as much pleasure from an outing to Yarmouth with the choir, or a show of magic in Norwich, as from a holiday with his family in Paris. Although he rubbed shoulders with many of the big names of the day, he found regular room in his diaries for simple, everyday observations;

Jan 1st, 1854 - Drove to take service at Hoe in a sleigh, the snow being too deep for wheels. Had some difficulty in getting through a drift where the horse was above his knees in snow. There were 19 communicants, and I can hardly tell how they got through the snow to church.

Jan 18th, 1855 - Notwithstanding the snow, there were several at Evensong, when I had the misfortune to lock one of the singing boys into the church. Luckily I heard his cries before I had gone too far away; a lump of plum cake soon appeasing him!

April 17th, 1859 - Buried Benjamin Tolladay at Hoe. He was nearly 100 years old - one of those righteous peasant patriarchs. With all our education and advancement, will the next generation to them be as good as they?

March 4th, 1862 (Shrove Tuesday) - The pancake bell was rung out from the steeple, as it has been from time immemorial on this day, an announcement, I presume,

that Lent was about to begin, and that shriving should not be neglected. I do not suppose that few people in the parish know that it means anything in particular.

May 19th, 1884 - Baptized the infant son of our organist, the father being 77 years of age!

Charlotte Atkyns (1758-1836)

Brave actress

A memorial to this female Scarlet Pimpernel is on the north wall of the nave of Ketteringham Church, a few miles from Norwich. She was an actress at Sheridan's Drury Lane Theatre, and Edward Atkyns, of Ketteringham Hall, fell in love with her when he saw her on the stage. They married, and travelled on the Continent, where Charlotte became close friends with the Queen of France, Marie Antoinette.

When the Queen was imprisoned and condemned to death, Charlotte tried to help her escape, disguising herself in scarlet coat, breeches and three cornered hat to gain an interview. But that was as far as Charlotte got. After her husband's death - and he had acted as a strong restraining influence - Charlotte spent a lot of money on wild schemes to rescue the poor little Dauphin. Again, she failed.

Her last years were spent in comparative poverty because she had helped so many others financially. The actress, who even disguised herself as a soldier of the National Guard in an effort to rescue the French queen during the French Revolution, died in Paris and lies in an unknown grave.

Dick Bagnall-Oakeley (1908-1974)

True all-rounder

Norfolk dialect expert, naturalist and teacher, he spent his early years at Hemsby, where his father was vicar. He was educated at Gresham's, in Holt, and read geography at Clare College, Cambridge. When he was 25 he was asked to "hold the fort for a fortnight" as a geography teacher at Gresham's. He accepted the

invitation - and stayed for the rest of his teaching career.

His skills were abundant and varied, and he represented the county at hockey, athletics and rifle shooting. But from childhood, natural history, ornithology in particular, was his first love.

He made himself an authority on migrant birds in North Norfolk, and he was an expert on capturing all wildlife and plant life on film. His informative yet humorous talks about natural history both on local television programmes and at lectures throughout the region made him a well-known figure.

Often he would break into the Norfolk dialect, which he loved and at which he was an expert. He feared it was disappearing as an older generation died and parts of their vocabulary were lost. He also wrote about natural history in numerous articles and in books, and he was invited to lecture throughout Britain and abroad. He served as president of the Norfolk Naturalists' Society, and was a member of the council of the Norfolk Naturalists' Trust.

In "A Tribute to a Norfolk Naturalist", Logie Bruce Lockhart describes Richard Percival Bagnall-Oakeley as "one of the last true all-rounders, an outstanding, if mildly eccentric, example of a species of Briton approaching extinction. His joie de vivre spilled over, so that everyone else felt better for it. Again and again his pupils and colleagues marvelled that he could excel in so many activities and still find time to be a genius in the classroom."

He collapsed and died at the wheel of his car in April 1974, while driving to Inverness, where he was to have given a lecture on ornithology.

Stanley Bagshaw (1914-1964)

Press giant

Outstanding Norfolk newspaper man - with a passion for Europe. His father presided over local affairs for the Norfolk News Company at Cromer, and Stanley and his brother Peter also decided to make their careers in the Press.

Stanley became fluent in at least six languages, and he built up a wide network of contacts throughout Europe. He arrived in Madrid on the very day the Spanish Civil War broke out, and he was in Czechoslovakia when Conrad Henlein was agitating for the return of the Sudetenland to Germany. With the outbreak of the Second World War he began his military career as a private soldier, but when his true talents were discovered, he was transferred to the Intelligence Corps. He followed Field Marshal Montgomery across North Africa and up through Europe, coming out with the rank of Lieutenant-Colonel and an award for gallantry.

With the arrival of peace, he returned to the Redwell Street office in Norwich, and worked his way up to the post of editor-in-chief of the Eastern Daily Press and its associated papers.

"We print both sides to every question, and our readers, whatever their basic beliefs, receive a balanced account of what is happening in the world." This did not imply a tendency towards parochialism. Indeed, when Kruschev and Bulganin made their famous visit to England, the EDP carried a leading article which he had written in Russian, and copies of the paper were sent to the Soviet Embassy and to the Kremlin. He formed the Norwich International Club in 1951.

He was only 50 when he died of leukaemia. One of his contemporaries said: "Stanley Bagshaw was a happy man. He had a gift for tongues and an even greater gift for friendship."

Thomas Baines (1820-1875)

News artist

Born in King's Lynn, he became an intrepid war journalist, or "news artist" as he was more correctly termed. His pictures were sketched as the battles raged and sent by runner and rider, by sailing ship and stage coach, to end up on the pages of the Illustrated London News many weeks after the original battle was won or lost.

Wanderlust took him to South Africa, where he turned his back on painting landscapes for elegant drawing rooms, and joined expeditions to explore the uncharted hinterland. In the meantime, the long-running Kaffir Wars were in progress, and Baines, with his penchant for recording everything he could, painted vivid battle scenes. These were brought to the attention of one of the generals who appointed him artist draughtsman of the armed forces. So he joined the ranks of the war journalists. He made many more expeditions including one to North West Australia in 1855.

His paintings and artistic records of the Dark Continent were to the Victorian, with his colonising zeal, what the satellite pictures of moon and planets are to the present generation. He died in Durban in 1875, and Edward Mohr wrote: "By profession an artist, he had become familiar with all those arts and contrivances by means of which life in the wilderness can be made pleasant. There was always something to be learnt from him."

John Betjeman (1906-1984)

Poet's link

John Betjeman, the most popular poet in this country since Kipling, was a regular visitor to Norfolk and had a strong personal link, a lifelong friendship with the Harrod family of Holt. In 1955 the man who was to become the people's Poet Laureate opened an exhibition of Osbert Lancaster's pictures in the Castle Museum in Norwich. In 1958 and 1968 he took part in the King's Lynn Festival. On the evening before the 1968 visit he was in Thetford for the first public performance of a new cycle of poems set to music by Mervyn Horder. In 1970, Sir John - knighted the year before - arrived in Norwich to tour in a day and a half all the city's medieval churches and in particular the two dozen marked down for redundancy at that time.

Thomas Bignold (1761-1835)

Union man!

Founder of one of the largest insurance organisations in the world, he moved to Norwich from Kent in 1783. He asked for one of the insurance offices in London to insure him against theft of his belongings on the coach journey between Westerham and Norwich. He was told that such a form of indemnity was unknown, untried and not insurable. "There is nothing that is uninsurable" he replied, "The question is merely would those who would fain be insured pay the price?".

In Norwich, Bignold soon urged the establishment of a fire insurance office. In 1792 he persuaded the Mayor to call a meeting of the citizens - and the Norwich General Assurance Company was formed. Its capital was £100,000 and it was to be wound up at the end of 30 years. Thomas Bignold was its secretary and ran it in his spare time. Five years later he left the Norwich General to set up another venture which was destined to become world famous. He got the support of 27 citizens, each subscribing only one pound to the general purse but giving a guarantee up to 1000 pounds against the risk of loss by fire to any of the other members. So the Norwich Union Fire Office was born in a modest way.

Thomas Bignold set up a separate office for life insurance and annuity business on similar mutual principles. He left Norwich to extend the business of the two insurance societies. His third son, Samuel, was appointed in his place, and the Bignold name continued to dominate Norwich Union until Sir Robert's retirement in 1964.

Thomas Bignold was buried in the churchyard at Old Catton, just outside Norwich. A creative and versatile man, perhaps his qualities are best summed up in the way he reacted to severe weather conditions in East Anglia in 1808. There were snowdrifts up to ten feet in many places. The Newmarket mail was held up for five days. Such conditions, not unnaturally, led to an unusual number of deaths. The perfect time to extend the Bignold business activities to life insurance.

Thomas Bilney (1495-1531)

Burned at stake

Born in the small parish of East Bilney, a few miles from East Dereham, he was burned at the stake in the "Lollards' Pit" in Norwich, close to the river at Bishop's Bridge. The movement known as Lollardy had emerged in the late 14th century, with members seeking more freedom of religious thought and the right to interpret the Bible for themselves. Although the movement was driven underground in the 15th century, a new wave of criticism of the Roman Catholic church began in the early 16th century, and the burning of Norfolk Lollards continued.

Bilney met his fate just before the final break with Rome. Educated at Cambridge, he was ordained a priest in 1519. Although he largely accepted the Rome position, including the Pope's supremacy, he did not believe in the mediation of saints between man and God, or in the worship of relics. His preaching was welcome in many places, but Wolsey chased him down for heresy, and he was found guilty. After a year's imprisonment in the tower, he was released and went back to Cambridge. He agonised with his conscience, and in the end chose preaching - and death.

He was not allowed to use churches, so he preached in the open air until he arrived in Norwich, where Bishop Nykke arrested him and had him tried, degraded and sentenced. The Bishop was later charged with carrying out the execution without authority of the state and his property was confiscated. Bilney's ashes were taken back to his home village, but precisely where they are now only God knows. It is recorded that Dr Warner, a rector of Winterton, accompanied Bilney to the stake...

"Dr Warner came to him to bid him farewell, who spake but few words for weeping; upon whom the said Thomas Bilney did most gently smile, and inclined his body to speak to him a few words of thanks; and the last were these:'Farewell, good Master Doctor! and pray for me!'. And so Warner departed without any answer, sobbing and weeping."

A small, insignificant-looking man, Thomas Bilney became a brave warrior as one of the faithful forerunners of the English Reformation.

Billy Bishop (1913-1986)

Nature warden

Billy Bishop was warden on the Cley Marshes nature reserve for 42 years. He took over in 1937 from his grandfather Robert, who had been the first warden there after it was bought by the Norfolk Naturalists' Trust in 1926. Billy Bishop attracted bitterns, bearded tits and avocets back to breed at Cley, and also created a series of shallow lagoons called scrapes which encouraged more wildlife activity and helped make the reserve one of the most popular bird-spotting areas in the country. He died aged 73 in 1986.

Henry Blogg (1876-1954)

Lifeboat hero

Coxswain of the Cromer lifeboat for 38 years, with 53 years service in all, he was described as "one of the bravest men who lived" by Viscount Templewood, president of the Cromer branch of the Royal National

Lifeboat Institution. No other lifeboatman won as many medals as Henry Blogg. Three times he won the gold medal, the lifeboatman's VC, and four times the silver medal. Among other awards were the George Cross and the British Empire Medal

He joined the Cromer lifeboat in 1894, when he was 18. He became coxswain at 33 and continued in that role until he retired in 1947 at the age of 71. During his years of service the Cromer boat went out 387 times and saved 873 lives.

In his biography, "Henry Blogg of Cromer, The Greatest of the Lifeboatmen", Cyril Jolly describes the funeral of Thursday June 17th 1954, when 1400 people packed the parish church... "Outside another thousand waited in the churchyard and formed a square five deep around the low church wall. Nothing like this had happened around this coast before. It was unforgettable. The splendid church, with its weathered flints and storm-worn masonry, towered protectively above the mourners standing in sorrow and silent homage. It seemed not a mere building but an old, understanding friend. From within came the low pealing of the organ leading the congregation in the hymn "Oh God Our Help In Ages Past". Between the verses, and above the sounds of a strangely subdued town, came the low, continuous rumble of the sea - the sea that had fed Blogg, and fought Blogg, and now seemed to murmur its last mighty tribute to him."

Henry Blogg hated fuss and refused to talk about his exploits. He was the most reticent of men, and some maintain the most telling comment he ever made was one sentence of rebuke to a gushing woman visitor who came up to him on the promenade when a summer storm was driving great breakers up the beach and exclaimed: "Oh, Mr Blogg! Isn't that beautiful!".

"No, my dear" said old Blogg, quietly, "That ent bewtiful, thass cruel".

Francis Blomefield (1705-1752)

Rector historian

Norfolk historian and Rector of Fersfield, near Diss, from 1729 until his death. He printed his "History of Norfolk" on his own press at Fersfield Rectory. "I don't care one farthing if I print my work in a manner to my own liking ... I don't print (I thank God for it) for my bread, having a comfortable subsistence independent of all men."

Even so, Blomefield got into financial troubles, partly because he was also a hunting man and kept his own pack of hounds. When he died at the age of 47, halfway through writing the third volume of his history, he was so much in debt his executors would not act but handed over the administration of his estate to his two chief creditors. He died from smallpox, caught on a visit to

London for research. He had refused to be inoculated and thus avoid an evil sent by God. He lies buried in the chancel of Fersfield church.

It was through Blomefield that the Paston Letters came to light. He was invited to Oxnead in 1735, and in the country house built by William Paston he found the precious letters, the earliest great collection of family letters in English, among the ancient tomes, document boxes and ledgers. (See also Margaret Paston).

Blomefield began collecting material for his Norfolk history while he was still at school in Thetford, but it was not until he became rector of his home village that the work began to take shape. He sent out a comprehensive questionnaire to more than 200 people, and travelled extensively to collect and verify information. He got as far as page 678 of the third volume before he was struck down by smallpox, and his history of the county was carried to its conclusion by Charles Parkyn, Rector of Oxborough, near Swaffham.

Boadicea (or Boudicca)(died AD 61)

Warrior queen

One of the first "real" people in Norfolk history, she remains one of the area's most potent heroines, emerging, rightly or wrongly, as a symbol of a struggle for freedom. Her rebellion against the Romans was a blood soaked affair. The Queen of the Iceni, whose daughters had been raped by the invaders, while she had suffered a public lashing, called for resistance and revenge as she roused her Norfolk-based tribe with her outstanding gifts of oratory.

Terrifying images of the warrior queen have flowered into folklore over the centuries, with pictures of flashing blades on the wheels of her chariot, and it is hard to know where fact fades into fable. "She was of the largest size, most terrible in aspect, most savage of countenance and harsh voice; having a profusion of yellow hair which fell down to her hips and wearing a large golden collar" is how Greek writer Cassio Dio described her.

She had nothing but contempt for the Romans: "They can't stand hunger, thirst, cold or heat as we can - they are men who bathe in warm waters, eat artificial dainties, drink unmixed wine, anoint themselves with myrrh, sleep on soft couches with boys for bedfellows - boys past their prime at that - and are slaves to a lyre-player, and a poor one too!". But the Romans were too strong and too well organised after Boadicea's armies had sacked the main Roman settlements of Colchester, London and St Albans.

The Romans claimed to have killed 80,000 Britons while losing only 400 legionaries. It is thought the warrior queen poisoned her daughters before taking poison herself. There are many reports and rumours as to Boadicea's final resting place, but none have any real substance. It has been suggested that Peddars Way was built soon after the revolt to give the legions quick access to the tribal lands of the Iceni when necessary.

A flavour of what life might have been like in her reign can be found at the reconstructed Iceni village at an ancient history site at Cockley Cley, near Swaffham. A Victorian statue of the Iceni Queen is on Westminster Bridge in London.

Anne Boleyn (1507-1536)

Lost her head

Her ghost is said to haunt Blickling Hall, near Aylsham, and it is difficult to separate fable from fact with regard to her connection with one of the country's most beautiful houses. She was the second wife of Henry VIII and mother of Elizabeth I. In order to marry her Henry divorced his first wife, Catherine of Aragon, thus breaking with the Roman Catholic Church and providing the occasion for the official Reformation in England.

Henry and Anne Boleyn were married secretly in January 1533. She produced no male heir and was convicted of adultery and beheaded on May 19th 1536. According to tradition, Anne spent holidays at Blickling as a child with her parents, brother and sister. In one of the rooms in the present hall there is a wooden plaque dated circa 1780 which states that she was born at Blickling. It was formerly the seat of the Boleyn or Bullen family.

Once Anne was dead stories soon started circulating about strange happenings in the Blickling neighbourhood. A coach drawn by headless horses had galloped to the doors of the hall, and inside sat the form of a young woman, also headless, with her bleeding head upon her lap. As the years went by the apparition was said to repeat its appearances on the anniversary of her death. Occasionally the coach was said to be driven by her father, Sir Thomas Boleyn. The legend has been embroidered, but there can be little doubt that Anne Boleyn knew Blickling well before her untimely end.

Blickling Hall now belongs to the National Trust. The original house was built by Sir Nicholas Dagworth in the 14th century. It was later bought by Sir John Fastolf who sold it to Geoffrey Boleyn, Anne's great-grandfather. Sir Henry Hobart built the house that stands today.

Edmund Bonner

Cottage museum

Edmund Bonner was Rector of East Dereham from 1534 until 1540. He later became Bishop of London and gained notoriety for burning about 200 people at the stake during the heresy trials in Mary Tudor's reign. Bishop Bonner's Cottages in Dereham were built in 1502, and are now occupied by the local antiquarian society's museum.

George Borrow (1803-1881)

Gipsy champion

Born at Dumpling Green in East Dereham, and baptised in the parish church, he refers to the town with affection in his writings. His mother was the daughter of a farmer at Dumpling Green and his father a sergeant in the West Norfolk Militia. Even as a child George travelled a great deal. "Lavengro" and "Romany Rye" blend fact and fantasy, reflecting his own eccentric scholar-gipsy personality.

As an agent for the British Bible Society he was in Spain at the time of a ferocious civil war. His successful book "The Bible in Spain" combined vivid contemporary reporting with the charm of a picaresque novel. "Lavengro", first published in 1851, is half-autobiography, half-novel, underlining Borrow's love of the unconventional, the life on the open road. It is in this volume that his most quoted line about Norwich being "a fine city" first appeared. "Romany Rye" continues the story of a fine horseman, boxer, walker, linguist, writer, dreamer...

Borrow suffered from what psychiatrists now call manic depression and what he referred to as "the horrors". But he was a fine descriptive writer, although the scenes and characters he evoked were often the creation of a retrospective fancy.

Borrow spent a fair amount of his life locally after being educated at Norwich Grammar School. He lived in Great Yarmouth, Lowestoft and Oulton Broad during his married years. East Dereham, the town of his youth, was later described by the writer as having "clean but narrow streets branching out from the modest market place; with old-fashioned houses, with here and there a roof of venerable thatch."

One story goes that while he was still at school he persuaded three other boys to run away to Yarmouth with him. With few provisions and no money the quartet set off - but they were caught before they reached Acle and brought back to Norwich. George Borrow's taste for travel and adventure did not suffer unduly. He is buried at West Brompton Cemetery, Kensington, London, next to his wife.

Noel Boston (1910-1966)

Full of vigour

Round, rosy and genial, Noel Boston was one of the most gifted clergymen to make a mark in Norfolk. So closely did he identify himself with the area it is easy to forget that he was a Warwickshire man. Ordained in 1935, he moved to Norwich three years later as Minor Canon and Precentor of the Cathedral, and chaplain and divinity lecturer at Norwich Training College for Teachers. Then he became Vicar of Catton, where he served until the end of the war when he moved to East Dereham. He was appointed Rural Dean, the youngest in the diocese. He was Vicar of Dereham for 20 colourful years.

Antiquary, musician, preacher, broadcaster, lecturer and organiser he certainly lived with gusto. He collected instruments of the old church bands that preceded organs, like the large, curly, bassoon-like serpent, and he could play them all. He collected ancient firearms on which he was also a leading authority. The national society of the Friends of Ancient English Churches grew out of a discussion in his vicarage in 1949, and so, in 1963, did the Norfolk Society, conceived as a union of civic societies for the whole county.

The Norfolk Record Society published in that year Noel Boston's "Musical History of Norwich Cathedral". He was a Fellow of the Society of Antiquaries, a member of the Central Council for the Care of Churches and a director of the "English Hymnal". He belonged to numerous local organisations, and was a natural gift to radio and television.

On leaving Dereham in 1965 he became a residentiary canon at Bury St Edmund's Cathedral. He died at 55 while on holiday in Northumberland. When he left Dereham his congregation praised him above all for his "cheerfulness, vigour and enthusiasm". He had hoped to return to Norfolk, and had begun the restoration of the ancient manor and grounds of Buxton Lamas, where he planned to make his home on his retirement.

Thomas Browne (1605-1682)

Knighted scholar

Writer and scholar, Browne was a successful physician who, except for his years of schooling in Oxford and Europe, spent his life in Norwich. He was knighted in 1671 by Charles II as a steadfast Royalist famous for his antiquarian scholarship. He was a great lover of language - he was the first to notice Norfolk had a dialect of its own - and his prose, so rich in exotic coinages and striking images, is one of the most remarkable accomplishments in English literature.

He is reckoned to be at his best when he treats themes that allow the full display of his personality, such as religion in "Religio Medici" and oblivion in "Hydriotaphia or Urn Burial". He settled in Norwich in 1637 and married Dorothy Mileham and they had 12 children. He became involved in the notorious Bury witch trial of 1662 when the judge asked for his expert opinion. Had the children been bewitched or not? Browne considered they had - and two old widows from Lowestoft were hanged four days later. The trial was thoroughly documented and quoted frequently as a precedent during the Salem witch trials in Massachusetts in 1692.

Sir Thomas Browne's statue on Hay Hill in Norwich was unveiled in 1904. He sits deep in thought on a plinth - with his back to a modern store.

His memorial is nearby in the sanctuary of St Peter Mancroft Church. In 1840, while another grave was being prepared, his coffin was accidentally smashed open. His skull, hair and the broken coffin plate were removed and sold to a local chemist, Robert Fitch. They were later acquired by a Dr Lubbock, who presented the skull to the Norfolk and Norwich Hospital. It remained there until after an undignified squabble over the cost, it was returned to St Peter Mancroft Church in 1922. It was reinterred in a specially made casket, with full burial rites, which referred to it as being aged 317 years.

John Bowman (born 1879)

First manager

John Bowman was Norwich City Football Club's first professional manager. He was appointed in March 1905, when City turned professional and joined the Southern League. Born in Middlesborough in 1879, he played for Port Vale and Stoke City before joining Queen's Park Rangers, first as a player and later as secretary/manager. On his arrival in Norfolk to take up a similar post with Norwich he was asked if he had any previous knowledge of the club ... "Well, I knew of City's existence, for in my schooldays geography was a favourite subject of mine, and I have since heard of the canaries." This is thought to be the first time the popular pastime of the day, rearing and showing canaries, had been linked to Norwich City. The club then still played in blue and white. Bowman resigned in June 1907; the transfer of star forward David Ross to Manchester City, divisions in the boardroom and financial problems took the shine off two good seasons at the start of Norwich City's professional life.

Fanny Burney (1752-1840)

Literary mark

Born in King's Lynn, she was one of the first novelists to deal with the experiences of a young girl coming into contact with the social world. She was a rather backward child but started scribbling stories before she reached her teens. She burned all that she had written, and then secretly wrote her first novel "Evelina". It had been her good fortune to sit quietly in a  corner of a drawing-room filled with the talk of such men as Edward Burke, Sir Joshua Reynolds and Dr Johnson.

Fanny collected a mere £20 for "Evelina" even though it was a great success. (A copy of the book fetched £4000 in 1930). For her next book, "Cecilia", she received £250. Then on being introduced to society she unhappily took a post as keeper of the robes to Queen Charlotte, and led the life of a lady's maid. She gave it up when her health suffered, and she settled at Mickleham where she met some French refugees. She married one of them, General D'Arblay, and they went to France where the General died soon after Waterloo. Fanny came back to her own land and lived quietly and simply until 1840. Considering that she could not read the alphabet when she was eight, she had made a bold mark in the literary world.

She lived as a child in Lynn in a house facing the west end of St Margaret's Church, where her father was organist. She later spent summers in the town after her family had returned to London. Fanny rose early for walks in the fields around Lynn because there was nobody about then; it was impossible to do likewise in London "for fear of robbers - but here everybody is known, and one has nothing to apprehend." However, she loathed the social life of Lynn's upper class families: "Such a set of tittle tattle, prittle prattle visitants! Oh fear! I am sick of the ceremony and fuss of these dull people!"

Thomas Fowell Buxton (1788-1845)

Freed the slaves

Thomas Fowell Buxton spent his last years at Northrepps Hall in North Norfolk. He married Hannah Gurney of Earlham, and succeeded William Wilberforce as leader of the anti-slavery party. He was made a baronet in 1840, and buried at Overstrand when he died five years later. In London a subscription was started, headed by 50 pounds from Prince Albert, to place a full length statue of him in Westminster Abbey where it stands next to that of his old friend Wilberforce. Meanwhile, the freed slaves erected a bust of him in Sierra Leone.

Harry Carter (1907-1983)

Vivid signs

Scores of Norfolk towns and villages bear vivid testimony to the talent and generosity of sign artist Harry Carter. For over half a century he designed and made an array of signs instantly recognisable as his work, some handed over as gifts and many others carved for little or no cost. The first sign he made was the famous one standing proudly at the entrance to Swaffham Market. It depicts the story of John Chapman, the pedlar reputed to have found a great treasure as a result of a dream. The sign was made in 1929 and given to the town by Harry Carter.

After that he made scores of signs, not only for Norfolk but also for communities in other countries as well. Shortly after the Coronation of 1953 an approach was made to the Queen, offering a sign for one of the villages on the Sandringham Estate. Her Majesty chose West Newton, and the sign was carved at Hamond's

Grammar School in Swaffham, where he was art and woodwork master for 30 years. One boy elected from each form accompanied the sign when it was presented to the Queen in January 1955. In exchange the Sandringham agent arranged for a good supply of royal oak to be provided for the school's honours boards.

During the Second World War, Harry Carter was a camouflage artist for the Army and the RAF. A cousin to Howard Carter, the famous Egyptologist who was brought up in Swaffham, Harry also had his own dance band. A truly colourful character, with his curly locks and bow tie, his craft has left so pleasant and distinctive an imprint on the face of Norfolk.

Born and educated in London, he was trained at the Slade College of Art. Before the war he was an artist and designer for companies such as Marples and

Sandersons. When he retired from making signs in 1981, he said: "I have made them because I love doing them. It has been my hobby."

Howard Carter (1874-1939)

Tomb treasure

The man who grew up in Swaffham and uncovered a treasure of unimaginable magnificence - the tomb of the Egyptian boy king Tutankhamun, which had lain undisturbed for over three thousand years. Howard Carter led the work of excavation for over a decade, and described November 26th 1922, as "the day of days, the most wondrous that I have ever lived through." For it was then that he penetrated the doorway to the first chamber of the tomb and signalled one of the most important finds in archaeological history.

It was during his early years in Swaffham that he developed his artistic talent and interest in ancient Egypt under the patronage of Lord Amherst, a wealthy local businessman. It was through Amherst and his family that Carter was able to travel to Egypt where his draughtsmanship skills were quickly noticed and he was employed to record the wall paintings of recently opened tombs. He soon moved on to excavate the tombs himself and so he met his future patron, Lord Carnarvon. They had violent arguments, but made their peace before Caernarvon's death in April 1923.

At the exact moment of Caernarvon's death an unexplained power failure left Cairo in darkness. His death, and Carter's illness soon after, fuelled stories of the "Curse of the Pharaohs"; the idea was given further credence by the fact that by 1929 over a dozen people connected with the Valley of the Kings and the tomb of the boy king had died. Carter dismissed the talk as a "libellous invention". It took him until 1933 to complete the removal of the crypt's objects. He spent his final years in great pain, writing, drawing and lecturing. He died at his London home in 1939, and was buried at Putney.

Carter was a solitary and difficult man whose background and education left him ill-prepared for the deluge of publicity that followed his amazing find. But he was a man of great dedication and talent whose contribution to our knowledge of ancient Egypt deserves far more praise. He was never honoured by his country or the many institutions that benefitted from the discovery of Tutankhamun's tomb.

Edith Cavell (1865-1915)

Died a heroine

Born in Swardeston, near Norwich, where her father was vicar for nearly half a century, Nurse Edith Cavell was shot by the Germans for helping Allied soldiers to escape during the First World War. She was working under the protection of the Red Cross and knew that she was breaking the rules. But she followed her Christian principles and gladly risked her life. "She died like a heroine" said the British chaplain who visited her shortly before she was shot.

She began her working life as a governess but switched to nursing after being inspired by a hospital she saw on a holiday to Austria and Bavaria. After training and working in London she went to Brussels to set up a school for nurses, and this became a Red Cross hospital when war broke out. Edith became part of an underground lifeline for Allied soldiers. She took photographs of the men for false Belgian passports, gave them food and money and sent them to the Dutch border. Her fate was sealed when two members of the escape route team were arrested. The Germans carried out the execution hastily, just a day after her conviction. There was a great outcry and the recruitment rate doubled in the two months after her death.

At first she was buried at the rifle range where she died, but in 1919 her body was exhumed and returned to England. A special service was held in Westminster Abbey, but her body was returned to Norfolk by popular demand. She is buried at a spot called Life's Green outside Norwich Cathedral, and nearby, in front of the Maid's Head Hotel, is a monument to her. There is a service in her honour with a flower festival at Swardeston Church on the Sunday nearest to the date of her execution - October 12th 1915.

Her famous last words: "I am not afraid or apprehensive. I have seen death so often that it does not seem strange or terrible .... standing as I do in view of God and Eternity, I realise that patriotism is not enough. I must have no hatred or bitterness towards anyone."

Mary Chapman (1647-1724)

Care pioneer

Her progressive ideas helped to lay the foundations of modern mental care. Mary was 35 when she became the second wife of the Rev Samuel Chapman, and one of the bonds that drew them together was the fact that both had relatives who were mentally sick, and both were deeply concerned for their welfare. When Samuel died he left in his will a sum of money to build "a hospital for the habitation of poor lunatics, and not for natural born fools or idiots."

Mary accepted the task of building only the second mental hospital in the country. The Bethel Hospital in Norwich opened its doors to its first patients in 1713, and it was a most progressive institution for its time. For a start, the idea of mental unbalance being an illness was not generally acceptable. In most parts of the country lunatics were regarded as little better than criminals.

Patients in Norwich were given facilities for recreation and worship, and the Bethel kept up with modern developments. Gas lighting was installed in the 1840s and the telephone and electricity before 1900. The whole emphasis was on cure, and the hospital was reporting a rate of recovery in excess of sixty per cent at the start of this century.

Mary Chapman lived in the hospital until her death in 1724 and is buried in Thorpe St Andrew churchyard.

Today the Bethel Hospital is used to treat children and adolescents with psychiatric problems.

William Clarke (1877-1925)

Breckland man

Naturalist and historian William George Clarke gave the region its name of Breckland in an article in the "Naturalists' Journal" of 1894. Such was his passion for the area he was reluctant to spend a night away from the warrens, and would shave with a prehistoric flint implement he found near Brandon.

He was born in Yorkshire of East Anglian parents and moved to Thetford as a boy. He was educated, like Tom Paine, at the Grammar School, and at 14 he was apprenticed to his father as a printer. By 1897 he had become a journalist on the staff of the Norwich Mercury. He later became president of the Norfolk and Norwich Naturalists' Society, honorary secretary of the Prehistoric Society of East Anglia and a fellow of the Geological Society.

W G Clarke, as he was invariably known, simply loved Breckland. He picked up flints with ease and some fine specimens found by him are to be seen in the British Museum as well as at Thetford and Norwich. His knowledge of botany and ornithology was so great he could say how many varieties of wild flowers there might be on one particular stretch of heath, and what species of birds and how many pairs had nested there during all the years he had known it.

He was deeply upset during the First World War at the destruction of rare flowers and the scaring of birds by the establishment of the large training camp near Thetford. He was spared the much more drastic changes which came to Breckland in more recent times. His book "In Breckland Wilds" stands as a portrait of an area which now only survives in a mutilated state.

Colin Chapman (1928-1982)

Lotus founder

Founded Lotus Cars in London - and moved the company to Norfolk a decade later. He died in 1982 at the age of 54. Various sites were considered when Lotus started to look for a green field location away from a heavily industrialised area. In the end, Mr Chapman opted for the former second world war airfield at Hethel a few miles from Norwich, partly because of his own love of flying. The Hethel factory opened in July 1966, and Mr Chapman was awarded the CBE for services to export three years later. Lotus cars are now sold in over 20 countries. General Motors acquired a controlling interest in Lotus in 1986.

William Cobbett (1762-1835)

Horseback chronicler

Cobbett included Norfolk in his series of tours of the English countryside on horseback - his famous "Rural Rides". He set out from London on October 30th, 1821, reaching Norfolk in early December. He was most impressed and left full of admiration and respect "for this county of excellent farmers and hearty, open and spirited men. The Norfolk people are quick and smart in their motions and in their speaking. Very neat and trim in all their farming concerns and very skilful. Their land is good, their roads are level, and the bottom of their soil is dry, to be sure; and these are great advantages; but they are diligent and make the most of everything."

Edward Coke (died 1634)

Legal giant

Edward Coke, born in Mileham, became one of the outstanding figures in the legal world of his time. He was first made Recorder of Norwich, then of London. He was then appointed Solicitor General to Queen Elizabeth I and Speaker of the House of Commons. He was subsequently chosen Attorney General, in which office he continued under King James, who appointed him Chief Justice of both benches. He died Lord Chief Justice of the King's Bench in 1634, at the age of 83. An altar monument in the chancel of Tittleshall church records his honours and virtues.

Thomas Coke (1754-1842)

Farming fame

The best managed estate in the late 19th century was undoubtedly that of the Cokes of Holkham. As well as a long parliamentary career - he represented Norfolk or Derby for 56 years - Thomas William Coke, later Earl of Leicester, took a keen interest in agriculture. "Turnip" Townshend, on the nearby Raynham Estate, has been credited with the invention of crop rotation. Coke was responsible for popularising what was known as the Norfolk Four Course.

Landlords such as Coke and Townshend introduced tenancy agreements that made the four course rotation compulsory, including the growing of turnips. Hay, straw and root crops all found their way back to the soil in the yard manure. The growing of beans, peas, lucerne, sainfoin and clover, once in the rotation, also helped to enrich the soil. A monument in Holkham Park shows some of the things that made Coke famous. Bas-reliefs represent the sheep shearings and the creation of

an irrigation scheme; while a Devon longhorn bull, a Southdown sheep, a seed drill and a plough take their places on top. On the corners of the base Holkham also becomes the pivot round which the social life of the county revolved.

The column was set up by public subscription in 1850 as a memorial to the man who succeeded to the estate in 1776 and was created Earl of Leicester in 1837. Coke said of Holkham that when he first knew it two rabbits could be seen fighting for one blade of grass, and he transformed it into a rich and fertile heritage.

He was a popular personality, and a cheerful song called "Barley Mung" celebrates some of his caring qualities:

Coke little reeks of low or high,
Coats fine or jackets rarely worn;
The landlord of Holkham ne'er looks down
On the humble growers of barley corn.

(See also "Turnip" Townshend")

Jeremiah Colman (1830-1898)

Father figure

Mustard magnate and benevolent employer, Jeremiah James Colman moved the business from Stoke Holy Cross, outside the city, to Carrow in Norwich so goods could be shipped down the river. He built the first mustard mill, and Colmans has been the best known name in the mustard business ever since. The Victorians used it in mustard plasters, mustard baths, mustard emetics. Tradition has it that the biggest profits come from what is left on the plate!

In 1856 Jeremiah and his wife started the Carrow social welfare scheme. There was no state education and no provision of meals for workers. Canteens were unknown, state schools had yet to come. So the Colmans started a school for the children of their employees. It began with 22 youngsters, parents paying a penny a week for the first child and a ha'penny a week for subsequent children. The school had 234 pupils by 1870. The Colmans crowned this practical welfare work by starting a nursing service. Jeremiah Colman became known as the industrial patriarch in excelsis. His personality dominated the works. He was firm but just and kindly - the father of his people. The tradition was continued with the family producing men and women of outstanding abilities. In 1938 the company was amalgamated with Reckitts.

When Jeremiah was buried in 1898 shops were closed and traffic came to a standstill ... an immense procession, with a cavalcade of carriages behind the hearse, a column of great J & J Colman wagons drawn by the firm's matchless horses, loaded high with wreaths and tributes of every size and description from every conceivable source. Behind that came walking some 1200 of the workpeople of Carrow.

Jeremiah James and his wife Caroline had six children, all of whom followed in their parents' footsteps in being dedicated to both Carrow and Norwich.

Astley Cooper (1768-1841)

Top surgeon

Born in Brooke, near Norwich, where his father was curate, he became one of the greatest surgeons of his time. Surgery was in his blood, for his grandfather and uncle were surgeons of note and when he was only 21 Astley Paston Cooper was appointed demonstrator at St Thomas' Hospital, a post he filled brilliantly. He divided anatomy from surgery in his lecturing and found discussion of his own cases was of far more interest to his students than theory.

As his fame as a lecturer grew his private practice flourished until it became the largest any surgeon has ever had. In 1802 he was elected Fellow of the Royal Society and his income in one year was 21,000 pounds - a far cry from the five guineas he netted in his first year. For one operation carried out at the peak of his fame, a rich West Indian planter tossed him a thousand guineas - in his nightcap! He became Professor of Comparative Anatomy to the Royal College of Surgeons, and in 1817 performed his historic operation of tying the abdominal aorta for aneurysm.

He received a baronetcy for operating on George IV, who had a small tumour in the scalp, and many other honours and successes followed. When he died at 73, Sir Astley was buried in the chapel at Guy's, and a statue was erected to him in St Paul's. A street in his home village of Brooke now bears his name - Astley Cooper Place - and in September 1968 there were special bicentenary celebrations.

John Sell Cotman (1782-1842)

Inspiring brush

He ranks as one of the greatest local artists even though much of his best work was done in London and Yorkshire. Born in Norwich he was educated at the city's free grammar school. He left for London to develop his art. On returning to Norwich in 1806, his ambitions largely frustrated, he joined the Norwich Society of Artists, exhibited for the first time a year later and made his presence felt.

Cotman was producing masterpieces from boyhood, brilliant water-colours painted with direct, clean transparent washes put on in controlled, sharply defined masses giving decorative patterns, superb design, volume and depth. He appreciated that the essential beauty of water-colour is obtained by the reflection of light through the wash of colour from the paper.

The best collection of his work is in the Castle Museum in Norwich. His paintings achieved little popularity at the time, and Cotman became extremely disillusioned, gloom and despair alternating with periods of intense activity.

A wealthy Yarmouth banker and antiquarian, Dawson Turner, became his patron, and it was under his influence that between 1812 and 1818 Cotman published the first series of his Norfolk etchings - "The Architectural Antiquities of Norfolk". Soon after came "Engravings of Sepulchral Brasses in Norfolk", both key works for students of the county's churches. He also designed the weather vane for Knapton Church, in North Norfolk.

Cotman, though he painted comparatively few East Anglian scenes, has become the quintessential East Anglian artist, and remains one of the main inspirations to artists working in the region.

William Cowper (1731-1800)

Troubled poet

Buried at East Dereham, where he spent the last years of his troubled life, William Cowper is hailed as the poet of the religious revival of the 18th century. He was a literary pioneer in that he worked to bring poetry into the life of man, so rescuing it from being nothing more than a scholar's exercise ... "Give me a manly rough line with a deal of meaning in it, rather than a whole poem full of musical periods that have nothing but their oily smoothness to recommend them." He was described as the first poet to love nature entirely for its own sake, and he composed some of our most famous hymns - "Hark! my soul, it is the Lord" and "O, for a closer walk with God".

Many of Cowper's lines have become common English expressions without it being realised they have come from him: phrases like ... "the cups that cheer, but do not inebriate", "Variety's the very spice of life", "God made the country and man made the town" and "England, for all thy faults, I love thee still".

In Dereham Church a magnificent stained glass window commemorates Cowper, a man who, all his life, was gentle, quiet, withdrawn, unbalanced and disturbed. With the help of friends he was able to break fresh poetic grounds, from "The Ballad of John Gilpin" to the simple glories of the English countryside. Some hear in his verses the faint notes of the music of nature which later swelled into the majestic harmonies of Wordsworth.

It was in Olney, in Bedfordshire, that Cowper first found the friendship, retreat and protection he needed. He went to live with a Reverend Morley Unwin, his wife Mary and their family. When Unwin died, Cowper continued his friendship with Mary. Later, when they both had to be cared for, they moved to Norfolk. They became engaged to be married, but at once his insanity came on again. In the last few years of her life Mary suffered several strokes, and watching her fade was an added agony for the troubled poet. Part of the house where he and Mary lived in Dereham Market Place was demolished in 1874 to build a Congregational church bearing his name.

John Crome (1768-1821)

Norwich School

Founder and father-figure of the world-famous Norwich School of Painters. At 15 he was apprenticed to Mr Whistler, coach, house and sign painter in Norwich, and so learned at an early age to grind and mix colours and to apply oil paint to canvas or panel. Crome got a job as a drawing master and was befriended by Thomas Harvey of Catton, wealthy member of a notable Norwich family who had his own private gallery of masterpieces. Crome then obtained the post of drawing master to the influential Gurney family of Earlham.

In 1803 the Norwich Society was formed to instigate "An Enquiry into the Rise, Progress and Present State of Painting, Architecture and Sculpture, with a view to point out the Best Methods of Study to attain Greater Perfection in the Arts". That prepared the ground for the Norwich School of Painters which was to survive three generations of local artists. It was the first exhibition by a society of artists other than those held in London. In 1806 Crome exhibited his first two paintings at the Royal Academy. He was known as "Old Crome" by the time he was 43 for he had three sons, all of whom became painters.

In the magnificent large canvasses "Mousehold Heath" and "Poringland Oak", which both hang in the Tate, we see him in his prime. But in April 1821, while working on the preliminary sketch for the Yarmouth Water Frolic, he went down with a fever and died within a fortnight. There is a memorial to Crome in the church of St George, Colegate, in Norwich, where he was buried in the south aisle chapel. But his true memorials hang today all over the world, and there is a superb collection in the Norwich Castle Museum.

He was a fine technician, both in oils and water-colour, and had studied closely the great landscape painters of Holland and the Netherlands. Unlike Cotman, he was content to stay in Norwich although his outstanding talents would have allowed him to take London by storm.

William Crotch (1775-1847)

Child prodigy

When Mozart played before King George III he was seven years old. When William Crotch of Norwich did the same some years later he was just three and a half. His father's fondness for music had led him to build a small pipe organ for his house and to teach himself to play hymn tunes on it.

The child prodigy was taken on tour by his parents and proved a big success. He performed before London society and had audiences with the Prince Regent and George III, who was most impressed. Crotch went to Cambridge to study when he was 11 and his first composition was performed when he was 13. At Oxford, where he graduated in music, he was appointed a Professor of Music at St John's College at the age of 22. He taught for 50 years at Oxford and became first

Principal of the Royal Academy of Music when he was 47. A brilliant theorist, he was responsible for some useful innovations - and yet, ironically, his paintings and drawings are probably more esteemed than his music.

One of his musical pieces that is broadcast regularly is the Westminster Chimes, the tune that precedes the striking of Big Ben. Crotch is said to have based it on a figure from Handel's Messiah.

He is buried at Bishop's Hall, near Taunton, and his music is performed very rarely these days.

Harold Davidson (1876-1937)

"Prostitutes' Padre"

Rector of Stiffkey and Morston for 26 years, he was proud to be called the "Prostitutes' Padre". He began early to show the interest in fallen girls which led to his downfall. Before the First World War he made fortnightly visits to Paris in search of suitable girls to rescue. Throughout the 1920s he continued his mission in London, travelling there before dawn on Mondays and not returning until late on Saturdays. Investigators were hired to follow him and one of them extracted a scandalous story from a target of his missionary zeal.

Rose Ellis withdrew her accusations, but not in time to prevent Davidson publishing his full story in the Empire News. By now the Press was accusing him of immoral practices with over a thousand girls. His fame grew and the congregation at Stiffkey rose to 500. In February 1932, a coachload from Bournemouth travelled to Norfolk to hear him preach.

Davidson was brought before the Consistory Court, sitting in Westminster. His trial lasted over four months.

When the chancellor retired to consider his summing-up, Davidson went back to Stiffkey and promptly ejected a clergyman sent to minister in his absence. When the court found him guilty on all five charges he went to Blackpool and sat in a barrel for 14 hours a day to raise money for his appeal. On the day of his ceremonial defrocking in Norwich Cathedral, he continually interrupted the Bishop. In the summer of 1935, Davidson and his daughter Pamela returned to Blackpool to enter adjoining fasting cages. They were arrested and charged with attempted suicide, but the charge failed and Davidson was awarded £382 damages against Blackpool Corporation.

At Skegness Amusement Park in the summer of 1937, when speaking to the public from inside a lions' cage, he was attacked by a lion and suffered bad injuries to his head and neck. He died two days later, and is buried in Stiffkey churchyard.

William D'Oyley (1745-1814)

Safety pioneer

William D'Oyley was most unusual for his time - he cared about road safety. Born at Bergh Apton, he became the curate of Stratton St Michael and Flordon with Hapton. He remained a poor man all his life but luckily for several villages, and for Norwich, he put his own interests last.

When he noticed a danger spot, like too steep a descent or a nasty bend, he mounted his horse and rode to all villages around. He asked for subscriptions and used the money to remove the hazards. He collected enough money to have a hilly road near Tasburgh made less steep. One day in Norwich he noted the bottleneck in Brigg Street before it widened into the Haymarket and the Market Place. He rode an estimated 12,000 miles collecting money from villages to the east, south and west of the city in order to improve the road.

This poor parson rode the equivalent of 15 times the distance from Land's End to John O' Groats on horseback and he didn't cut down the travelling in later life. He did not see many results for all his work, for road improvements were a long time coming. He collected more than £400 but died the following year. The money was paid into a trust fund and was used when the work was eventually carried out - 35 years later. A plaque commemorating the work of this road safety pioneer is fixed to the wall of Debenhams store in Norwich.

Daniel Defoe (1660-1731)

Famous visitor

Defoe, the celebrated author of "Robinson Crusoe" and "Moll Flanders", was also a great traveller. His "Tour Through the Eastern Counties" was originally published in 1724, the first instalment of his journey throughout Great Britain. In Norfolk he saw "the face of diligence spread over the whole county" and was told there were 120,000 people employed in woollen and silk manufacture in Norwich alone. Along the coast he heard of smuggling, "a trade carried on with much less honesty than advantage". Defoe condemned the scandal of Castle Rising which "with perhaps not ten families in it, yet sends two members to Parliament, being as many as the city of Norwich itself or any town in the kingdom."

Bill Ecclestone (1901-1985)

The only Chairman

William Ecclestone, whose career as a Great Yarmouth councillor and alderman spanned three decades, made his mark on the history of local politics - becoming the only chairman of the reshaped district council in 1973. He had been mayor of the old county borough in 1965, and his long public services were honoured by the award of the freedom of the borough. The retired architect turned popular historian and published a number of books reflecting the development of the area in which he lived. One of his main loves was archaeology, and he was president of the town's society. Arthur William Ecclestone joined E Lacon & Co. as an assistant surveyor in 1920 and rose to become a director of the brewery.

Bill Edrich (1916-1986)

Cricketing legend

William John Edrich was born in Lingwood, a member of Norfolk's most famous cricketing family. Brothers Brian, Eric and Geoffrey and cousin John all played the first-class game. "A farmer's boy came to Lord's to reap such a rich harvest" - that's how Bill summed himself up in one of his books, "Cricket Heritage". He became a legend on the international stage despite having his career cut short by the Second World War, during which his bravery as a bomber pilot won him the DFC.

After cutting his teeth with Norfolk, for whom he made his debut at 16, he went on to represent Middlesex and England with distinction. During his first-class career he hit 36,965 runs, took 479 wickets and claimed 526 catches. In 1938 he amassed over 1,000 runs before the end of May. But it was his series of famous partnerships with Denis Compton that brought colour to those grey, austere days just after the war. In a golden 1947 they made 7,355 runs together; the Edrich total was 3,539 including 12 centuries.

Bill returned to captain Norfolk in 1959 and led then until 1968. Between 1932 and 1936 he scored 2,160 runs for Norfolk and took 119 wickets. By the end of his second spell with the county, from 1959 until 1971, those figures stood at 8,308 and 417 respectively. As a Bracondale schoolboy in Norwich young Bill once grabbed all ten wickets against Norwich High School, and he hit an unbeaten 149 against City of Norwich School.

He made his Football League debut for Spurs against Blackpool in 1935, but six years later he was forced out of the game by strained knee ligaments. He married five times. Former Middlesex colleague John Warr, invited to one of Bill's weddings, recalled being told he needed an invitation to get in.

"Invitation? I've got a season ticket to Bill's weddings!" he replied.

George Edwards (1850-1933)

Son of the soil

One of the key characters behind the formation of the National Union of Agricultural Workers, he was born in Marsham, near Aylsham, in abject poverty. Working on the land almost as soon as he could walk - bird scaring in the fields seven days a week for the princely sum of a shilling - he received no education worth talking about. He was still unable to read or write when he married, but wife Charlotte became his teacher. When the call came to George to organise the labourers she said: "You make the effort, I'll make the sacrifice". At the age of 70

he was returned as Labour MP for the South Norfolk constituency. When he made his maiden speech one newspaper referred to his "earth-clodden sentences".

"From Crow Scaring to Westminster" is George's stirring story. Knight alderman, magistrate and Methodist preacher .... but he never lost the common touch in his pioneering work for rural trade unionism. When the first union collapsed he went lecturing and, later, turned his back on the land. Then came another call. "I said to my wife, 'I do wish these poor people could find someone to lead them. I don't feel equal to the task.' Her reply was 'You must try. There is no-one else who will.'" The early days of his struggles on their behalf brought him as much bitterness as the latter days brought honour.

He became an MP in 1920. He was knighted in 1930. His last appearance in public was at a meeting of Walsingham Rural District Council a few weeks before his death. He was feeling unwell but had a reason for going. His last public utterance was a protest against the eviction of a man, his wife and family. In the Land Worker of January, 1934, George Clarke's poetic tribute was among many:

To George

In poverty you came to earth,
But poverty produced a man of sterling worth
To ease the burden from another's back
You purpose firm and courage did not lack
Although we lay you low and dust to dust,
To carry on the work we will, we must
Your harness laid aside, finished your toil
Peacefully sleep - a good son of the soil.

He is buried in Fakenham Cemetery, where an annual service of remembrance is held. Connections with the town are represented by a plough on the town sign.

Albert Einstein (1879-1955)

Visiting genius

Einstein, brilliant mathematician and physicist famous for his theory of relativity, brought his genius on a short-stay visit to Norfolk in 1933. He was sacked from his post as Director of Theoretical Physics at the Kaiser Wilhelm Institute in Berlin because he was a Jew. He fled from Nazi threats and found sanctuary for a while in a wooden hut on Roughton Heath, near Cromer, before he went on to America. His Norfolk host was Commander Locker Lampson, the local MP, who had this country retreat at Roughton. Einstein stayed in the hut most of the time with a "minder" on permanent duty outside with a rifle. Herbert Eastoe, a retired gamekeeper from the Gunton estate, had that role.

Ted Ellis (1909-1986)

People's naturalist

"Having feasted my senses on the wonders of nature since I was a toddler, the countryside wherever I have happened to be has been a never-failing source of

interest and delight." That is how naturalist and broadcaster Ted Ellis summed up his career shortly before his death in 1986.

Born in Guernsey of Norfolk parents he was fascinated from childhood by the "rich adventures" of discovering the natural world. He came to Norfolk when he was ten and a few years later, in Yarmouth, he met the great naturalist Arthur Patterson, who was to be such an influence through his knowledge of wildlife and birds. The old man maintained that a true naturalist should always be ready to share his pleasure with others. If communication was Patterson's gospel, it was certainly the Ellis gift.

Ted was Keeper of Natural History at the Castle Museum in Norwich from 1928 until 1956. For 40 years he lived with his family at Wheatfen Broad, Surlingham, in a remote cottage by a reedy wilderness. He wrote a regular column for the Eastern Daily Press as well as articles for The Guardian. From the 1960s he found a new audience as a popular radio and television broadcaster. An honorary degree of Doctor of Science was conferred by the University of East Anglia in 1970.

When Ted Ellis died Dr Tony Irwin, Keeper of Natural History at Norwich Castle Museum, said: "I don't think there is going to be his like again. His breadth of knowledge has never been equalled, and our knowledge of natural history in Norfolk is down to Ted." He was a pioneer in the field of conservation long before it became fashionable. He became a celebrity but remained a modest man. Self-taught scientist, he had the joy of nature constantly shining in his eyes. He was buried in an ancient churchyard among his beloved marshes. He wanted a country village funeral, and after a short, simple service at St. Mary's Church, Surlingham, it was appropriate that family and friends should walk the few hundred yards along a country track to Ted's final resting place in St Saviour's churchyard, a peaceful corner of Norfolk where nobody had been buried for 200 years.

Three months later there was a thanksgiving service in Norwich Cathedral. A congregation of 800 included eminent scientists from all over the world.

Whitwell Elwin (1816-1899)

Village cathedral

William Elwin created one of the most extraordinary churches in East Anglia in the small village of Booton, near Reepham. It is known as "the Cathedral of the Fields", a many-pinnacled building, startling and unorthodox, with twin towers set cornerwise. Elwin, who was Booton's rector for 50 years, began rebuilding the village church in the 1870s. His design included details from as far afield as Venice and the early Coptic churches of Egypt. St Michael's is a magnificent monument to Victorian enthusiasm. Elwin was also editor of the Quarterly Review and friend of many contemporary writers, including Scott and Thackeray.

Peter Emerson (1856-1936)

Broads photographer

"As a means of artistic expression the camera is second only to the brush .... All we ask is that the results should be fairly judged by the only true standard - nature." So said Peter Henry Emerson, one of the most outstanding Broads photographers. Born in Cuba and trained as a physician in England, he gave up practising in 1886 for many other interests, most notably for the rural life of the Fenlands and the Broads.

One of Emerson's techniques was the use of differential focussing to achieve soft outlines. He was one of the first photographers to publish extensive portfolios of his work and claimed "Birds, Beasts and Fishes of the Norfolk Broadlands", published in 1895, was the first book on natural history entirely illustrated by photographs.

"Life And Landscape on the Norfolk Broads" (with T R Goodall, 1886) shows his work at its best. He was constantly working at two levels simultaneously. While he was busy "creating art" with his camera, he was also meticulously recording every aspect of rural life just as a naturalist would collect specimens. He even penetrated the highly-organised poaching rings, and went so far as to argue their case in "Pictures of East Anglian Life".

Emerson's photographic contemporaries, who helped leave us a splendid record of life on East Anglia's waterways, were George Christopher Davies, first clerk to Norfolk County Council, and John Payne Jennings, who came under contract to the Eastern Railway Company to take the photographs which adorned their railway carriages.

Emerson's books often contained statistical appendices on meteorology, agriculture and bird and game sightings. He had the sort of fertile mind that could produce "A Son of the Fens", a novel in Norfolk dialect; "Suggested Amended Billiard Rules for Amateur Players"; and "Naturalist Photography for Students of the Art". A man of great intelligence and independent means.

Thomas Erpingham (1357-1428)

Shakespeare salute

Sir Thomas Erpingham was a Norfolk knight who led the English archers at Agincourt in 1415 - and earned his place in Shakespeare's list of characters. About 9,000 troops under Henry V defeated 60,000 French. The flower of the French nobility were either killed or taken prisoner. The Erpingham Gate, leading from Tombland into the Cathedral Close in Norwich, is the gallant knight's thanksgiving. His kneeling figure in stone, his sword at his side, is in the gable. The turrets at either side are panelled with shields which show the coats of arms of Sir Thomas and his two wives.

He was one of the faithful few who risked their life and fortune for John of Gaunt's son, Bolingbroke. He was one of the little group who went over to France to the disinherited prince, and one of the few who set sail with him in the summer of 1399 for Ravenspur and kept him company in the thrilling drama which ended in the coronation of Henry IV. Sixteen years after landing at Ravenspur, Sir Thomas comes to the king's tent on the night before Agincourt, breaking in on the conference between Henry, Bedford and Gloucester:

Henry   *Good morrow, old Sir Thomas Erpingham;*
               A good soft pillow for that good white head
               Were better than a churlish turf of France.

Erpingham   *Not so, my liege; this lodging likes me better,*
               Since I may say "Now lie I like a king."

The king takes the old man's cloak because the night is chilly and he is to walk around the camp. Sir Thomas offers to accompany him, but Henry says:

              No, my good knight,
               Go with my brothers to my lords of England
              I and my bosom must debate awhile,
              And then I would no other company.

Erpingham   *The Lord in Heaven bless thee, noble Harry!*

Henry   *God-a-mercy, old heart, thou speakest cheerfully.*

George Ewart Evans (1911-1988)

Oral historian

George Ewart Evans, father of the oral history movement in East Anglia and doyen of its development throughout the country, died in Brooke, near Norwich, at 77 in January 1988. His books on the old ways of farming and the rural conditions of the region are an integral part of history libraries throughout this country and abroad. Born and educated among the miners of South Wales he moved to Suffolk in 1948 and spent his final years in Brooke. He came to realise that the old villagers were the last remnants of a rural culture destroyed by mechanisation. He set about collecting details of their lives and their language, making full use of tape recordings

William Faden (1750-1836)

Map milestone

Geographer to King George III and the Prince of Wales, William Faden published what is believed to be the first large-scale map of Norfolk on August 12th 1797. He also published many other maps during his career, a catalogue of his works in 1822 includes 350 items. Faden's spelling of some places on the Norfolk map, "planned from a scale of one inch to a statute mile", vary from that used today. For instance, the good folk of Silfield, near Wymondham, will note with some disquiet that Faden recorded their hamlet as "Sinfield".

Until the 1790s, the largest scale map of Norfolk was that surveyed by James Corbridge in 1730 at a scale of two miles to one inch. The accuracy and reliability of Faden's map appear to have varied with the features shown; scale inevitably imposed its limitations on the degree of detail that could be shown. It is, however, the first completed large-scale record of Norfolk - and the only one produced before the great changes that came with enclosure, population migration, the building of the railways and the impact of the motor car.

In the heading to the map Faden described himself as being the proprietor and publisher. The actual surveying was carried out for him by Thomas Donald and Thomas Milne as well as members of their staff. Perhaps because he was the owner of the map it has become known as Faden's Map - "Price to Subscribers is Two Guineas and a half, and to Non Subscribers, Three Guineas."

The map was printed in sections and totalled six sheets. Faden had already received awards for his maps of Hampshire and Sussex. Detailed as they were, his maps did not include parish boundaries, and it was not until publication of Bryant's Map of Norfolk during 1826 that these became officially known. In 1777, Faden published a North American Atlas which contained 34 maps. His plans also included those of the military operations of the American War of Independence. Faden was also one of the first cartographers to name the continent which had been known as the Southern Land Mass, Australia.

John Fastolf (1378-1459)

Castle builder

Son of a Norfolk squire, Sir John Fastolf was a professional soldier for much of his life. Although just a plain esquire at the start of Henry V's campaign, he rapidly earned promotion and under the Duke of Bedford he became one of the leading captains. He was personally involved in the Battle of Yernevil and all the battles around Orleans in 1429. He was made a Knight of the Garter, and made a fortune from successful warring - from wages, offices, plunder and ransoms.

He settled in Caister-on-Sea, near Yarmouth, in the castle he had built. He died on November 5th 1459. His wife died in 1446 and he had no surviving children - so John Paston, an old friend, was main beneficiary of his will. The validity of that will was questioned by Fastolf's other legal advisers and the disputes and litigations over his inheritance continued for 20 years.

Caister Castle took over 20 years to build and cost more than £6,000. It differed from most other great houses of the time in that it was built of brick and, with its slender tower and prominent moat, it resembled some of the castles of the Rhineland rather than those familiar to Fastolf in England and France.

When completed in 1454 it contained over 40 rooms, many of them lavishly decorated. The original layout of the castle consisted of two rectangular courtyards surrounded by a moat and connected by a drawbridge, the inner or western court dominated by a slender tower 90 feet high, still standing today.

Most of the famous Paston Letters were written at Caister. In 1469 the Duke of Norfolk besieged the castle with a force of 3,000 men. The defenders, with Margaret Paston in charge, held out for five weeks but were forced to surrender due to "sore lack of victuals and gunpowder." The castle was restored to the Paston family by the King in 1475.

Sir John Fastolf was one of the characters on whom Shakespeare based his Falstaff.

David Fisher (1760-1832)

Theatre family

Founder of the celebrated theatrical family company which for over half a century presented an unbroken succession of plays, operas, pantomimes and other entertainments in towns all over Norfolk and Suffolk. As a result of his importance as the company founder and of a long line of actors of the same name, he became known as David Fisher I, though strictly speaking he was the third in a direct line of eldest sons all named David Fisher.

He began his working life as a carpenter in the building trade, but he had a fine tenor voice and had a special talent for singing patriotic sea-songs. This soon led to his being invited to join the Norwich Theatre Company as a singer. He took to acting, married an actress, Elizabeth Burrell, and then made his biggest mark of all in management.

In the heydays of the company there were enough talented Fishers to take up to nine or ten parts in one evening's entertainment. In all, 18 of them acted on the family circuit. The founder died in 1832 at Dereham while the company was playing there. The Norfolk Chronicle paid this tribute: "As a manager he was esteemed, and by his indefatigable industry he has been enabled to leave his sons eleven theatres, many of which have been recently built and elegantly decorated. As an actor he displayed much talent. He was an affectionate parent and warm friend and in the strictest sense an honest, just and upright man."

In 1933 a gathering of Fisher descendants and theatre enthusiasts came together in Dereham churchyard to celebrate the renewal of his headstone.

A country-wide recession in the theatre led to the closing of the Fisher Circuit in 1844 and all the theatres were sold. But the sound basis on which they had been run meant that there were no debts to be settled at the end. The family went on to individual careers in the theatre and music.

Edward Fitzgerald (1808-1883)

Died at Merton

Author and translator, he died at Merton Rectory while on his annual visit to his friend George Crabbe, grandson of the poet Crabbe. Fitzgerald's translation of 'The Rubaiyat of Omar Khayyam' remains one of the most widely sold publications of all time.

Launcelot Fleming (1906-1990)

Team scheme

Bishop of Norwich from 1959 until 1971, Launcelot Fleming moved on to become Dean of Windsor and Domestic Chaplain to The Queen. He became Bishop of Portsmouth at the age of 43. Ten years later he was invited to exchange the smallest diocese for the second largest - Norwich. Unkindly known as "the dead see" with over 60 unfilled benefices, Norwich needed a man who would devote himself to his clergy, sorely in need of encouragement, a living wage and, in remote areas, an assurance they were not isolated and forgotten.

Faced with nine parishes in part of west Norfolk without an incumbent, he decided the only solution was to group isolated parishes together to be served by a team of three or four men in charge of eight or ten parishes. The idea met with early opposition, but eventually proved a success. He grasped other nettles. Bishop Fleming commissioned the Brooke Report, which looked at the problems of Norwich's 30-odd medieval churches and recommended that only a handful were needed for worship. Deep concern for young people led him to speak about their needs in the House of Lords, where as a scientist he continued to speak on the issues raised by nuclear and chemical warfare, the dangers to the environment and the future of Antarctica.

In 1934 he combined his two callings as chaplain and geologist to the British Graham Land Expedition. Here, in a long sledge journey to the furthest point south then reached, he made a notable contribution to the geology of Alexander Land and acted as priest-in-charge of the largest parish in the world, with only 15 companions as his critical parishioners.

One of the attractions of coming to Norwich was the new University of East Anglia. His Cambridge experience was invaluable - he studied geology at Trinity Hall - and since it had been decided there should be no theological faculty and no formal provision for organised religion at the UEA, Bishop Fleming was instrumental in the building of the Chaplaincy Centre, open to Christians and non-Christians alike.

Robert Forby (died 1825)

Man of words

Forby died five years before the publication of his "Vocabulary of East Anglia" in 1830, still a constant source of reference and delight. Born in Stoke Ferry, he went to school in King's Lynn and on to Caius College, Cambridge, from where he graduated in 1781. He held livings in Horningtoft, Barton Bendish, Wereham and, finally, Fincham. He became the Rector of Fincham in 1801 and held the post until his death. His famous vocabulary, reprinted in more recent years, was "an attempt to record the vulgar tongue of the twin sister counties, Norfolk and Suffolk, as it existed in the last twenty years of the 18th century, and still exists; with proof of its antiquity from etymology and authority." With over 2000 words and phrases it was the biggest collection made. Forby suggested "Such collections are not only curious but useful, and might be made of public and general interest."

Eric Fowler (1909-1981)

Mardle magic

Regarded by many as the most able and authoritative writer ever to work for the Eastern Daily Press. For 35 years his Wednesday morning essays, written under the pseudonym of Jonathan Mardle, delighted a wide and devoted readership.

He was an authority on Norfolk dialect, speaking and writing it with native resource and humour, and collections of his Mardle essays were also published. In his introduction to "Wednesday Mornings", a selection of the essays published in 1956, R W Ketton-Cremer, the Norfolk scholar and writer, said: "In this transitional period of our local history, we are fortunate that a writer with so lively a perception of scene and circumstance is observing and recording it all."

Eric Fowler was born in Queen's Road, Norwich, the son of a coal merchant. He joined the Eastern Daily Press in 1925, straight from Bracondale School in the city. He joined the Royal Norfolk territorials and was called up on the outbreak of war, spending over three years in the Indian Army. On being demobbed in 1946 with the rank of captain, he returned to the EDP and soon began writing the Jonathan Mardle column, which was to become one of the most distinguished expressions of English regional journalism. Made an MBE in 1968 for services to journalism, he retired from the newspaper staff in 1974, an occasion marked by the city and county at a unique gathering in the City Hall, a "function of honour" when leaders of local life paid tribute to his work.

The Wednesday "Mardles" were to survive this watershed, and he continued to delight his readers until the autumn of 1981. "What appeals to me most about East Anglia is the people. People are happy to live here and are proud of it. They've got roots" he wrote just before he died.

Peter Roberts, former editor of the Eastern Daily Press, said of Eric Fowler: "He achieved the distinction of having thousands and thousands of friends right through the region who never met him but gathered comfort, stimulation and provocation from all the articles that have appeared from his pen."

Elizabeth Fry (1780-1845)

Prison reforms

She was one of the twelve children of John and Catherine Gurney of Earlham Hall, near Norwich. Her father joined his brother as a partner in the Norwich Bank, established in 1770. Elizabeth - known as Betsy - suffered from nervous depression and low spirits in her youth, but became a noted promoter of wide-ranging prison reforms, particularly in the treatment of female prisoners.

A young Quaker, Joseph Fry, whom she had met in London, hurried to Earlham to woo her ardently. She refused him twice, but at length Joseph placed his watch and chain on the white garden seat among the flower beds of Earlham Park. "If Betsy leaves the watch on the seat she does not love me; if she picks it up, then she will marry me" said Joseph. As her sisters hid in the surrounding laurel bushes and peeped, she picked up the watch.

Stephen Grellet was the other man who had a big influence on her life. He visited Newgate Prison and was so horrified at what he saw in the women's quarters he went to capable, sensible Elizabeth Fry and enlisted her help. She changed it from a world of vice and horror to one of quiet, clean cells, freshly swept and whitewashed, and for stone pillows she introduced clean straw bedding.

As the prison horrors subsided in England, she turned her attention to the Continent. She visited the prisons and the princes alternately of each country, and all made her welcome. In some cases the kings and queens became her devoted friends and shed tears of sadness at her departure. Elizabeth Fry's "Memoirs" were published in 1847 - two years after her death.

Saint Fursey (died AD 648)

Influential visions

After Saint Columba, Saint Fursey is probably the best known of the Irish monastic missionaries abroad in the early Middle Ages. He first came to England some time after 630 and was welcomed by King Sigbert of the East Angles, who was encouraging the work of Saint Felix of Dunwich at this time. Fursey established a monastery at Burgh Castle, near Yarmouth, ministered from there for about ten years and then passed over into Gaul. He founded a monastery at Lagny, near Paris, and died at Mezerolles while on a journey. He was buried at Peronne, where his tomb became a place of pilgrimage and the monastery there an Irish centre.

Fursey is thought to have built his Burgh Castle monastery within the shelter of the north-east corner of the Roman walls, bringing Christianity for the first time to this part of East Anglia. Fursey's buildings were of wood and plaster, so little of them survived into modern times. However, in 1958 Charles Green carried out an investigation on behalf of the Ministry of Works and discovered post holes and some painted plaster to bear out the written evidence of a religious settlement here. It was not until 500 years later that the first church was built and dedicated to Saint Peter and Saint Paul. A Celtic stone cross was erected in the churchyard in 1897 in memory of Saint Fursey.

Bede says Fursey was "renowned for his words and works, outstanding in goodness", and Bede relates the visions of the unseen world of spirits, good and evil, which account for much of Fursey's fame. From time to time he fell into a trance-like state when he saw such things as the fires of falsehood, covetousness, discord and injustice lying in wait to consume the world. These visions had a big influence on the religious thought of Western Europe in the later Middle Ages, notably as expressed in Dante's "Divine Comedy".

Jack Gedge (1886-1986)

Last wherryman

Jack Gedge of Swafield, in North Norfolk, was the last of the old Norfolk wherrymen. He died at 100 in 1986, having started work on the wherries when Queen Victoria was on the throne. Born at Worstead, he was the third generation of his family to take up a life on the Broads. Both his grandfather, who lived to be 99, and his father were wherrymen.

Nathaniel Gill (1606-1669)

Defiant streak

A keen Royalist, he was sequestered from his living at Burgh, near Aylsham, in 1643. But for the next seven years he defiantly, and remarkably, remained there, continuing to marry and baptise his parishioners. He even kept the parish registers, so the name of his Puritan replacement is unknown.

Eventually, Nathaniel Gill was driven away to Bungay, still with the registers, but he returned to Burgh at the Restoration, when he made this entry:

"Nath. Gill (after seventeen years of sequestration, by traytors, rebels, Anabaptists, Quakers and Presbyterians) was restored to his rectory at Burrough and preached on Christmas Day 1660."

Later he also held the nearby living at Aylsham, but retained Burgh, where he is buried.

Sarah Glover (1786-1867)

Sound of music

Daughter of a Norwich clergyman, Sarah Ann Glover created the "Tonic-Sol-Fa" system which achieved remarkable results with untrained singers. As she became interested in music, she began to consider the possibility of finding a simple method of teaching both sight-reading and sight-singing.

She started to teach from her own scale chart, which resembled a ladder and was later to be called a modulator. To modulate means to change from one key to another during the course of a piece of music, such a change being accomplished by a continuous musical means - that is, not simply by starting afresh in another key. Almost at once Sarah found she could get better results by using her new method at the school she ran with her sister off Colegate Street in Norwich. She went on to teach singing at Lakenham School and also formed classes at Pakefield School and among children of the Norwich workhouse.

Even so, her work remained unknown outside local circles until 1841 when a young Congregational minister, the Rev John Curwen, was trying to find a simple way of teaching schools and church congregations to sing music, not only at sight but in tune. His enquiries brought him to Sarah Glover's school. He was impressed, and simplified and then commercialised her original idea. She lived to see Sol-Fa classes springing up all over the country, and overseas as well. Between them they decided that what

had been known as the "Norwich Sol-Fa System" would become the "Tonic Sol-Fa System", the name being still in existence today.

Aware of the problems of introducing her system into schools without supervision by an experienced musician, or musical instrument readily available, Sarah devised a simple keyboard instrument, limited to the range of children's voices, which she called her harmonicon. This was equipped with a device enabling the less-accomplished teacher to fix the key note and then identify the other notes of any major or minor key.

Sarah died in Malvern, Worcestershire, and one of the honours in her name is a memorial stone in the Tonic-Sol-Fa College in Forest Gate, East London, founded by John Curwen. Perhaps the easiest way of saluting Sarah Ann Glover is to sing that song from "The Sound of Music" - the one that starts "Doe, a deer, a female deer, Ray, a drop of golden sun". Those sounds, and the me, fah, soh, la, te, doh which follow form the Tonic-Sol-Fa.

Sidney Grapes (1888-1958)

The Boy John

The most endearing of local characters, Sidney Grapes made his mark as a rustic comedian at local concerts and dinners. But he will be most fondly remembered for the Boy John letters he sent to the Eastern Daily Press from 1946 until his death in 1958.

Sidney lived all his life in the Broadland village of Potter Heigham, where he ran a garage business. The letters were composed by a countryman who wrote as he spoke and spelt as he pleased, and featured the Boy John, Granfar, Aunt Agatha and the scandalous Oul Mrs W---. Perhaps the letters were more eagerly anticipated because they were infrequent. Sidney was pressed to become a regular weekly contributor, but he was as wary of the blandishments of journalism as he was of the professional stage.

Many readers "cheated" and always went to the P.S. first for Aunt Agatha's latest example of homespun philosophy - P.S. Aunt Agatha she say, "The more you say, the less people remember." Collections of the Boy John letters have sold in their thousands over the years, and retain their freshness simply because of the way they were drawn from the heart of Norfolk village life. In his address at the dedication service at Potter

Heigham Church on Sunday November 23rd 1958, the Bishop of Norwich, the Rt Rev Percy Herbert, said: "It is not given to many writers to create fictitious characters that are so alive, and that once met will never be forgotten...To read those letters is really to be enriched, and then to go on our way with the new courage that they breathe all the time, and a new joy in our hearts that we should be alive....He was not only an astonishingly fine natural humorist, he was an incomparable teller of good stories."

P.S. One year, a few weeks before Christmas, Sidney Grapes put this notice in his garage window at Potter Heigham: "A Happy Christmas to all my customers whot hev paid their bills, and a prosperous New Year to them whot hent."

Wilfred Grenfell (1865-1940)

Pioneer in snow

Famous throughout the world as "Grenfell of Labrador", this active and practical man forged close links with Gorleston after arriving on the East Coast in January 1889. He soon became a champion of the deep sea fishermen and lived at Cliff House in Gorleston, and later in the southern portion of the Cliff Hotel where there is a plaque stating he was there from 1892 until 1898. Wilfred Grenfell was the first doctor of the Royal National Mission for Deep Sea Fishermen. He left Norfolk to sail a small hospital ship to Labrador; the ketch *Albert* was built at Fellows' yard in Southtown, Great Yarmouth.

So he sacrificed a promising career as a surgeon for the life of a pioneer, spending nearly 50 years in the far North with the Eskimos, Indians and fisherfolk of Labrador. He was honoured by many universities and societies in Britain, Canada and the United States, and was knighted in 1927. He made long journeys by dog team from his ship, organising the building of hospitals, first-aid stations and children's homes. He encouraged the growing of vegetables to combat the deficiency diseases, and in his first summer there treated 900 patients.

One Easter, when driving across a frozen bay to reach a boy who was very ill, the weather became rough and broke up the ice. He was thrown into the water with his dogs. He cut loose the sledge and crawled on to a pan of ice. He killed three of the dogs, skinned them and used their coats to keep himself warm. Next day he hoisted a distress signal and was rescued by fishermen.

Returning to Gorleston after his voyages, he took an active part in local affairs and used to swim summer and winter from the beach at the foot of the cliffs. Born in Cheshire, he died from heart disease at his home in Charlotte, Vermont, USA in October 1940. The ketch *Albert*, in which he set sail for Labrador finished her life fishing. On May 25th 1968, just off Greenland in a strong wind, she lost her propeller and sprang a leak. A Norwegian fishing vessel went to help and took off her crew of 17. The *Albert* drifted onto an ice pack and became a total loss.

Thomas Gresham (1519-1579)

Finance expert

The Greshams, in their public works while living and by their wealth after their deaths, conferred lasting benefits on their county and their nation. Thomas was the son of Sir Richard Gresham, the Lord Mayor of London who was born in Holt in 1485. Thomas traded with the Low Countries, acting there as king's merchant for Edward VI. While living in Antwerp he bought munitions of war for the king, and kept his ministers informed about Continental developments in relation to the fear of attack.

As an agent of the English Government he obtained in 1552 some very important intercepted letters from Mary, Queen of Scots, to the French king. On the accession of Elizabeth, Thomas was asked to look after the country's finances and overseas trade. She also knighted him. In 1564, Sir Thomas offered to build, at his own expense, a "Burse" or Exchange for the merchants of London. The Royal Exchange was destroyed in the Great Fire of 1666, was rebuilt and burnt down again in 1888.

Sir Thomas greatly increased the influence of England as a Continental power. He reformed the country's finances and hampered Spain's threats, which culminated in the dispatch of the Armada to its destruction in 1588.

John Gresham, Thomas' uncle, converted his mansion house in Holt into a free grammar school in the 1550s, the management of which he confided to the Fishmongers Company. Gresham's School was "for the education of 50 Free scholars, to be chosen from the town of Holt and its neighbourhood, and instructed by a master and usher in reading, writing, arithmetic, English grammar, and in the Latin and Greek languages."

Gresham's is now a flourishing co-educational school. The Greshams are also perpetuated in the name of the village a few miles from Holt.

Henry Rider Haggard (1856-1925)

Radical squire

Born in Bradenham, near East Dereham, he wrote 50 books, including those epic adventures "King Solomon's Mines" and "She". The closest friend of his later years, Rudyard Kipling, admitted openly his envious admiration of Haggard's fertile imagination. As a young man he raised the British flag over Pretoria when Britain annexed the Transvaal Boer Republic. In later years he became a radical, reforming squire in his native Norfolk where he farmed over 350 acres at Ditchingham and Bedingfield.

While he is best known as a prolific writer he had many other talents and ambitions. He sought changes in farming techniques with government action to help develop a system of smallholdings with a co-operative management. His reforms were considered too radical by the Conservative Party, for whom he once stood as a parliamentary  candidate, but were adopted in part several years later by the Liberals. There was also Haggard the public servant, who served on several royal commissions considering such subjects as coast erosion and afforestation, the settlement of the poor of industrial

England in the colonies and the state of the dominions, for which services he received his knighthood.

It was from his mother Ella that he drew his literary talents. She wrote poems and songs which were published in various journals.

Henry Rider Haggard is buried at Ditchingham, with a simple sentence on the stone:

Here lie the ashes of Henry Rider Haggard,
Knight Bachelor
Knight of the British Empire
Who with a Humble Heart Strove to Serve his Country.

A special window is dedicated to him in St Mary's, with vignettes of his African farm, the Pyramids and a view of Bungay from the Vineyard Hills close to his home, drawing together strands of his varied and colourful life.

Lilias Rider Haggard (1893-1968)

Original works

The youngest daughter of Sir Henry Rider Haggard, she inherited his writing talents, and her books on Norfolk are among the best the county has inspired. "Norfolk Life", "Norfolk Notebook" and "Country Scrapbook" are delightful selections of her articles for the Eastern Daily Press. However, the two books she saw in manuscript and prepared for publication in the 1930s are among the most original works in local literature.

"I Walked By Night" is the autobiography of a Norfolk poacher... "What is written here was born of an old

man's loneliness, as he sat in a little cottage perched high on a hill, overlooking the Waveney Valley, with no company but his dog." The second book she edited was "The Rabbit Skin Cap", a tale of a Norfolk countryman's youth, set on the borders between Norfolk and Suffolk.

In his survey of East Anglian Literature from Crabbe to Adrian Bell, published in 1982, Ted Goodwyn said: "Miss Rider Haggard faced a difficulty common to regional writers; the rendering of the vernacular - of dialect words and phrases, of pronunciation and spelling. Whatever the peculiarities, the writer's aim is always to retain, as far as possible, sufficient of these to give the sound and feeling of the local speech whilst not obscuring the meaning for the general reader. For Lilias Rider Haggard, the difficulty involved the whole of the text. The two books she edited and shaped are models of how this difficulty may not only be overcome, but turned to advantage through the body and colour of the vernacular."

Although she spent most of her life in the village of Ditchingham, Lilias had travelled with her father in Egypt and South Africa, and was awarded an MBE for nursing services during the First World War. She was a member of Norfolk County Council from 1949 to 1952, and in 1955 was elected President of the Norfolk Rural Craftsmen's Guild. Her biography of her father, "The Cloak That I Left", was published in 1951.

Robert Hales (1820-1863)

Gentle giant

Robert Hales, born in Somerton, near Great Yarmouth, developed into the biggest man known in the western world at the time, and became celebrated as a freak. He grew to 7ft 6in and in his prime measured 64in round the chest and 64in round the waist and weighed 33 stone. His father, a farmer, stood 6ft 6in, and his mother, who weighed 14 stone, had an ancestor, a warder of the Tower of London in Henry VIII's time, who was 8ft 8in tall.

As a boy, Robert worked on a wherry, but it simply wasn't big enough to take him as he continued to grow.

He joined the Navy and served for three and a half years before he was discharged. Now he had outgrown a ship. As the fame of Norfolk's gentle giant increased, people remarked not only upon his size but upon his pleasant and cheerful disposition. He was received at court by Queen Victoria and the Prince Consort and in France he was introduced to King Louis-Phillipe. He went to America in 1848 to join Barnum and Bailey's Circus, and during a rough Atlantic crossing he plunged into the sea to rescue a child who had been swept overboard.

Hales returned to England in 1851, becoming landlord of the Craven Head Inn in Drury Lane. He was again received by Queen Victoria and Prince Albert, and six royal youngsters were also there to marvel at him. But Hales' fortunes declined and he was reduced to selling the story of his life at a penny a time on Gentleman's Walk in Norwich. That life was cut short by consumption when he was 43, and he was buried in Somerton churchyard in a stone tomb.

Robin Harrison (1908-1986)

Nature column

Harrison was a well-known figure in the Great Yarmouth area, noted for his love of wildlife. He was a warden of the Breydon Water nature reserve, and contributed newspaper articles under the name of "Robin". He wrote and illustrated a weekly column for the Eastern Evening News for 50 years. He was appointed a Breydon warden by the Norfolk Naturalists' Trust and the Yarmouth Naturalists' Society, and for many years kept a houseboat on the north bank. He died at 78 in 1986 a few months after being presented with a glass goblet by Yarmouth mayor Jim Benson to mark his long service to nature in the area.

Luke Hansard (1752-1828)

Printing prize

Her Majesty's Stationery Office produces Hansard, the official report on the proceedings of the House of Commons. By coincidence, just a few hundred yards from the stationery office buildings in Norwich is the small church of St Mary's Coslany. Luke Hansard was born in this parish.

On leaving school he was apprenticed to printer Stephen White, who was also a painter, engraver, bookseller, stationer and boat builder. Young Hansard was willing and quick to learn, and he could soon manage typesetting, layout, presswork and engraving. The business prospered and Luke mastered every aspect of the trade. At 18 he went to seek his fortune in London with only a guinea in his pocket.

He soon found a post with a printing firm run by John Hughes, and by 22 he was a master printer in charge of the printing department. In 1774, Hughes landed the contract for printing the House of Commons Journal, an unofficial account of the proceedings written by Radical William Cobbett. He published 6000 copies at one shilling (5p) each. Cobbett was a turbulent fellow, often contemptuous of restrictive practices. This brought him a three-year prison sentence in 1810.

By then Luke Hansard had become one of the big names in the business. The boy who arrived in the capital with a guinea died worth £80,000. His son Thomas bought Cobbett's Journal when the MP was in financial trouble during his spell in prison. The business remained in the hands of the family until 1889 when it was taken over by the Stationery Office. The name of Hansard was officially adopted for their reports in 1943.

Luke Hansard is buried in the London church of St Giles-in-the-fields. In Norwich, a short street off

Fishergate by St Edmund's Church perpetuates the memory of the local boy who made good.

William Harborne (died 1617)

Glorious return

William Harborne, trader, traveller and the first English ambassador to the Ottoman Empire, was born in Great Yarmouth and died in Mundham in 1617. He is buried under the main aisle of St Peter's Church in Mundham. Not only did he stimulate trade, but he succeeded in setting free a host of Englishmen from captivity and in making safe the way for English ships in Turkish waters. Dressed as a Turk, he joined a caravan and reached Constantinople where he won the heart of the Sultan and returned home in glory bearing a royal letter to Queen Elizabeth.

James Haylett (1824-1907)

Famous line

Haylett was the lifeboatman responsible for one of the most telling lines in local seafaring history. At the opening of the inquest into the tragedy of the Caister lifeboat *Beauchamp* in November, 1901, with the loss of nine of the crew, it was suggested to him that the lifeboatmen could have given up their mission and have been returning to the beach. James Haylett replied in defiant tones: "Caister men never turn back!", a phrase synonymous with the spirit of the village crews ever since. For his part in the rescue of the three survivors, James Haylett was awarded the RNLI Gold Medal, which he received from King Edward VII at Sandringham House in January 1902.

Richard Hearne (1908 - 1979)

Mr Pastry

Richard Hearne, actor, entertainer and creator of children's television character Mr Pastry, was born in Lady Lane in Norwich, now called Esperanto Way, on the site occupied by the Central Library.

Tom and Kitty Higdon

Burston strike

In 1911 Tom and Kitty Higdon took up teaching posts in the South Norfolk village of Burston. They were soon accepted into the community, respected for their generosity and fairness towards the pupils and for the way they made lessons interesting. But Burston was a desperately poor community, with low wages and cramped housing, and the school premises were in an appalling condition.

When Tom Higdon became involved in trade union activities and the couple tried to improve conditions in the school they met fierce opposition from the Rev

Charles Tucker Eland, rector and chairman of the school governors, and self-appointed upholder of the social and economic status quo.

The events that followed, bizarre and ultimately violent, have become known as the Burston School Strike - the longest in English history. It was a strike started by children when their teachers were dismissed, and it lasted from April 1914, until just before the Second World War. It involved Socialist leaders and trade unionists across the country and captured the support of the radical press.

Born in 1869, the son of a Somerset labourer, Tom Higdon continued to teach at the Strike School until shortly before his death in 1939. Kitty, five years older than her husband, went into sad decline when Tom died. Several times she was found wandering the lanes at night, saying she was waiting for him to return home from a union meeting. She spent her final days in a home at Swainsthorpe, near Norwich, and died in 1946.

The Strike School is now a museum. Before moving to Burston, the Higdons had been teaching for eight years at another Norfolk school in the village of Wood Dalling about 40 miles away. Despite good reports from the school inspectors about their work, the Higdons were dismissed because of "friction" between them and the school managers.

Michael Home (born 1885)

Breckland novels

Michael Home (pseudonym of Christopher Bush) drew upon memories of his early years in Breckland for his main novels. Born at Hockham in 1885, son of the village pig-keeper and barber, he won a place at Thetford Grammar School and took a degree in modern languages at King's College, London. He saw active service in both world wars, and his Breckland novels appeared in the inter-war years. There is much in Home's stories about the bitter political conflict in rural life, deepened by religious and social differences. "God and the Rabbit", "In This Valley", "This String First"

and "The Harvest is Past" won Michael Home a place on the shelf reserved for the best East Anglian novelists.

William Hooker (1785-1865)

Kew Gardens

Born in Norwich, he became determined at an early age to devote his life to the study of natural history. He was still under 20 when he made his mark on the scientific world with the discovery of a rare moss near Norwich. This brought him to the attention of Sir James Smith, who suggested he took up botany.

For over 20 years William Hooker travelled the world at his own expense in pursuit of plants. An expanding family and bad debts forced him in 1820 to take a job for the first time as Regius Professor of Botany in Glasgow. He established a network of plant collectors throughout the world, and he was knighted for services to botanical science.

But his greatest honour was yet to come. For years his frequent correspondent, the Duke of Bedford, had campaigned for a national centre for botanical research, and he felt Hooker was the man to lead it. The Duke died before his dream was fulfilled, and it fell to his third son, Lord John Russell, to obtain Hooker's appointment in 1841 as director of the Royal Gardens at Kew, site of the new institution, that we continue to be able to visit today.

A museum was another of Hooker's innovations, along with access to the public and an exchange of specimens with other botanical gardens throughout the world. Hooker bequeathed to the nation his remarkable private collection, so vast it had to be housed in a mansion built for the King of Hanover. And he left a grand example of a successful man who invested in the future of natural resources.

Kew's role was much more than botanical research for science's sake. It was soon to repay the nation's investment. Britain's rise to power in the 18th and 19th centuries was linked to the development and use of a number of key plants, including the Para rubber plant. The Brazilians enjoyed a virtual monopoly on this substance, but Kew managed to have a few seeds smuggled out. Nurtured and cultivated at Kew, they were then introduced to plantations in Malaya, thus playing a significant role in building a new empire for the British.

Father Ignatius (1837-1908)

Dreams and visions

Joseph Leycester Lyne moved into a house on Elm Hill in Norwich in 1864. He was 27 and a man of dreams and visions. the house was to be "The Priory of St Mary and St Dunstan", and Joseph Lyne became Father Ignatius.

He was born in Barking, Essex, the son of a merchant, and felt even as a boy that he had been chosen for some divine purpose. He went to Scotland to take Holy Orders before moving to Norwich. A strict regime was imposed but the order grew as Ignatius looked for local converts. However, there was a great deal of friction and public hostility, and stories began circulating about "miracles". For instance, Ignatius was supposed to have put out a fire by making the sign of the Cross. The wooden head of Christ on a crucifix had been  seen to turn. He was an absolutely single-minded man and a brilliant preacher - but an abysmal businessman. His order grew discontented and after a long wrangle about money the building was sold and eventually became a carpenter's workshop.

Ignatius carried on elsewhere for another 42 years. There were riots when he preached in London, but his main achievement was the reviving of a monastery in

Llanthorny in the Brecon mountains. It flourished for a number of years but did not long survive his death.

Before he left Norwich he held some "spirit-stirring services, and that at St Andrew's Hall on the Sunday evening will long be remembered by the thousands who were present, for the address delivered was certainly of a most powerful and eloquent character."

There are many stories about strange happenings in Norwich while Ignatius pursued his autocratic path. A churchwarden, angered by Ignatius' cavalier attitude to church furniture, complained to the Bishop. Then he fell dead. The congregation, equally aggrieved, set out for Elm Hill to burn the monastery down. But we have been told a sudden, violent and unpredicted thunderstorm doused the flames and drove off the mob.

Thomas Ivory (1709-1779)

City creations

Ivory built the first Theatre Royal in Norwich. He was the city's leading builder and architect in the 18th century with the Assembly House and the Octagon Chapel among his outstanding creations. John Wesley called the Octagon Chapel "the most elegant meeting house in Europe", but rival clerics referred to it as "the Devil's cucumber frame". The first Theatre Royal opened in 1758 with the comedy "The Way of the World" presented by the Norwich Company of Comedians. At first known as the "Concert Hall", it was licensed as a theatre in 1768. The present Theatre Royal is the third to stand on or adjacent to the site. Thomas Ivory's son William designed the first buildings for the Norfolk and Norwich Hospital.

Augustus Jessop (1824-1914)

Rector writer

Jessop wrote a number of historical works centred on East Anglia. The most popular, "The Coming of the Friars", is a lively history of medieval life in the region. He was Rector of Scarning near East Dereham for over 30 years, and material for his collection of essays called

"Arcady For Better or Worse" was gleaned from his parishioners. Dr Jessopp was for 20 years head master of King Edward VI school in Norwich, which he transformed into a modern school of high repute before he took the living at Scarning.

Alfred Jodrell (died 1929)

Benevolent squire

Jodrell rebuilt the parish church at Glandford in North Norfolk, and nearly the whole village as well. Truly the benevolent squire he also sent the local children to school in Holt in a covered wagon, long before the authorities thought of such a scheme. He restored the church in memory of his mother, and adjoining the churchyard is a building erected to house Sir Alfred's collection of shells. It is now a museum open to the public. He inherited the baronetcy in 1882, and grew reluctant to leave the delectable Glaven valley. When he died in 1929, his body was placed in a coffin of plain oak without a nameplate, in accordance with his wishes. After resting in Glandford Church, lovingly restored between 1899 and 1906, the coffin was taken through Bayfield Park, past the Hall, his home, to Letheringsett.

W E Johns (1893-1968)

Biggles in Norfolk

The author of the Biggles adventure stories about a World War I fighter pilot picked up some of his flying knowledge in Norfolk. Cpt Johns lived for a time at Sporle before the First World War, and worked as a sanitary inspector for Swaffham Rural District Council. As a Yeomanry trooper in 1914 he was mobilised, and later transferred to the Royal Flying Corps at Narborough before going to France. Narborough is mentioned in "Biggles of the Camel Squadron".

Mother Julian (born 1343)

Divine revelations

Her book, "Revelations of Divine Love", was one of the first written by a woman in English. Very ill and expected to die as she received the last sacrament, she had a series of visions and made a miraculous recovery.

It was not uncommon in the Middle Ages for men and women to shut themselves away from the world to lead a life of prayer and meditation. Anchorites and anchoresses had to satisfy the bishop as to their purity of character. They were then taken to a secluded building to live, from which they emerged only on death.

In Norwich there were anchorages at most of the gates and bridges and in some of the churches. In an anchorage built next to St Julian's Church, off King Street, dwelt this lady who took the name of the church. Some believe Mother Julian was a nun from Carrow Abbey. After her divine revelations she went into seclusion at 30 years old. The cell had a window through which she could see part of the inside of the church. She kept the "Ancreen Riwle" of conduct for recluses, a copy of which can be seen in the British Museum. This allowed her to have a servant who would buy food and look after her. Her "Revelations" dealt with the likeness of God, His love of mankind, the nature of man and how one may come to God.

St Julian's Church was badly damaged during a bombing raid on Norwich in 1942. It has been well restored and the cell has been reconstructed. Julian's views on God as "our Mother" have led to her being adopted as patron of the movement for the ordination of women.

Will Kemp (died 1608)

Dance marathon

Actor and dancer, Will Kemp is famous for Morris dancing from London to Norwich in 1599. That exploit arose from a bet. He made a wager he could dance the Morris all the way and started out from the Mansion House.

A friend and colleague of another Will - Shakespeare, no less - he was accompanied by three people, Tom Sly, his taborer; William Bee, his manservant; and George Sprat, a sort of referee. Kemp was followed by large and enthusiastic crowds, and while the actual dancing took nine days the entire journey took about four weeks.

Travelling through Hingham, Barford and Earlham, he arrived at St Giles' gate. Finding the crowds smaller than expected, he rode to an inn and returned to the gate next morning when he entered in triumph. Kemp was feted like royalty. He was met by the Mayor, Roger Weld, who accompanied him to the churchyard of St John Maddermarket where he completed his "nine daies wonder" by leaping over the wall. There was a grand procession to the Market Place.

When Kemp died he was buried in St Saviour's Church, Southwark, where his epitaph reads:

Welcome from Norwich, Kempe all joy to see,
They safe return morriscoed lustily,
But alasse, how soon's thy morrice done!
When pipe and tabor, all thy friends be gone.
Then all thy triumphs, fraught with streams of mirth
Shall be caged up within a chest of earth:
Shall be? They are, th'ast danced thee out of breath
And now must make thy parting dance with death.

His name is kept to the fore in Norfolk by Kemp's Men, a Morris dancing group.

Margery Kempe (1373-1440)

Weeping wanderer

Her life is the first known autobiography in English literature. Born in King's Lynn, she was married at 20 and had 14 children before she evidently went out of her wits, had a vision like Paul's on the road to Damascus, and made a bargain with her husband that she would go on a pilgrimage.

She wandered, weeping and sobbing over England and Europe, and even to the Holy Land, so depressing with her groanings that every other pilgrim avoided her. She began her pilgrimage in 1414 and her sobs doubled in volume as she made her way to Mount Calvary. Margery returned to King's Lynn and her husband - but then sailed from Bristol to visit a saint's shrine in Spain.

She came back to preach in England before moving on to Danzig. She was getting an old lady now, but the difficult journey back through Germany to Calais and Dover had to be made mostly alone for other travellers would not put up with her ways and were ashamed to be seen with her.

She tramped to London and, standing in the streets in her sackcloth apron, decried the vice she saw all around. Then she dictated her remarkable story. As Margery did not know Latin or French she wrote in English. This is the book which for generations lay in the library of Pleasington Old Hall, the Lancashire home of a Roman Catholic family who may have received the book from the monks at the dissolution of the monasteries.

All the way through Margery referred to herself as "this creature". Eventually it was recognised as an exceptional story of amazing religious experiences and pilgrimages, and a social history of unique interest.

Robert Kett (1492-1549)

Rebel leader

The main causes of hardship and discomfort in Norfolk in the middle of the 16th century were economic and social. There was much raising of rents, but the biggest concern was over the enclosure of common land by the local gentry, which threatened the livelihood of the peasants. There had been widespread disorder and rioting in many counties in 1549, but it was only in Norfolk that the peasantry found a leader of outstanding quality.

Robert Kett was 57, a tanner by trade, and landowner in Wymondham. He became the champion of the common people, but made it clear he was not rebelling against the government in London; it was the local government in Norfolk he sought to reform. His petition to Edward VI was politely phrased, and throughout the rebellion he acted with restraint and moderation.

Kett made an indelible impression on the Norfolk of his day, dominating the affairs of the county and of Norwich for six weeks. He established an orderly camp on Mousehold Heath where he was joined by about 20,000 men. He led a successful attack on the city, defeated one royal army and severely mauled another. However, Kett's rebellion ended, inevitably, in defeat.

The Earl of Warwick was given command of a large force, some 10,000 men, and once Kett's supply lines had been severed and he had been forced to leave the safety of Mousehold, defeat was unavoidable. About 3,000 rebels died in the battle of Dussindale, a low valley just north of the city and now a large housing development. Kett was tried for treason, found guilty and hanged at Norwich Castle. His brother William was hanged from the tower of Wymondham Abbey.

In 1949, four centuries after the rebellion, the citizens of Norwich placed a commemorative plaque at the entrance to Norwich Castle:

"In reparation and honour to a noble and courageous leader in the struggles of the common people of England to escape from a servile life to the freedom of present conditions."

R W Ketton-Cremer (1906-1969)

Outstanding scholar

Robert Ketton-Cremer, who insisted he was a biographer rather than a historian, lived at Felbrigg Hall, in North Norfolk. He bequeathed the estate to the National Trust. Born in 1906, he was educated at Harrow and Oxford and wrote several books with local themes. "Norfolk In the Civil War", his celebrated portrait of a society in conflict, was first published in 1969, the year of his death. His study of the reactions of Norfolk families and individuals to the ferment of the 1640s underlined his reputation as an outstanding scholar.

Roger Le Strange (1616-1704)

Great adventures

Most famous member of the family so closely linked with the history of Hunstanton. He was born at Hunstanton Hall, the ancestral home, in the year that William Shakespeare died. Roger Le Strange died in London in his 88th year having experienced an amazing variety of adventures.

He declared he would face any hazard for the King, and in 1644 he tried to recapture King's Lynn from the Parliamentarians. His plans betrayed, Roger was sentenced to death and spent three years waiting for the sentence to be carried out. He escaped to the Continent and eventually returned to England to exchange the sword for the pen. At the Restoration he was put in charge of all the printing machines in England, and for many years he was the fiercest of pamphleteers, scurrilous as was the fashion of the time. He wrote a stinging attack on Milton, but is best remembered for starting one of the first newspapers, the Public Intelligence, and for his translation of Aesop's Fables, which he first gave to the world in English,

Roger Le Strange's private life was hardly a happy one. He did not marry until he was over 60, and the girl with whom he fell violently in love proved to be foolish and extravagant. It seems that Roger's notoriety was distasteful to many of his relatives. His enemies described him as "the scandal of a worthy family, who have long been ashamed of him."

But his literary projects were prolific and many of them of good quality. He died carrying into the reign of Queen Anne his memories of King Charles, Cromwell and the siege of Lynn.

Jenny Lind (1820-1887)

Swedish Nightingale

Founder of the children's hospital in Norwich which bears her name, Jenny Lind was the most brilliant singer of her day - as well as virtuous, high-minded and charitable. In 1847, when the "Swedish Nightingale" came to sing in Norwich at St Andrew's Hall, great opera singers were as popular as today's television stars and pop singers. Indeed, the country was swept by Jenny Lind fever, and Norwich had its share.

The city concert was postponed from Monday to Thursday because she had a cold. Her safe arrival at the Bishop's palace on the Tuesday evening was marked by a peal of the bells at St Peter Mancroft. Edward Stanley, the reforming Bishop of Norwich, invited her to stay at the palace for a week - and for this he was condemned by the censorious as if he had entertained Jezebel herself!

Jenny Lind gave two more concerts in Norwich in 1849, raising over £1200 which she wanted to be used to found some lasting charity for the poor of the city. Public baths and wash-houses were proposed at first, but the more imaginative idea of a local doctor prevailed.

The Jenny Lind Infirmary for Sick Children was founded in 1853. It started as a small hospital of a dozen beds in some houses in Pottergate, and the founder kept in touch for the rest of her life. She wrote in 1885: "Of all the money which God allowed me to give away when my poor throat could call an audience to listen to its production, none has borne a nobler or more genuine fruit than the Jenny Lind Hospital in Norwich."

In 1897 the local proceeds of Queen Victoria's Diamond Jubilee Fund were devoted to a new children's hospital in Unthank Road, perpetuating the name and spirit of its original benefactor. The hospital was demolished and replaced by a children's department in the Norfolk & Norwich Hospital in the 1970s. Jenny Lind also endowed a whole hospital in Liverpool and the wing of another in London. Mendelssohn called her the greatest singer of the century. Queen Victoria went into raptures about her. The Duke of Wellington invited her to stay with him. And Norwich won a special place in her heart.

Sydney Long (1870-1939)

Trust Founder

Founder of the Norfolk Naturalists' Trust, Sydney Herbert Long was born at Wells-next-the-Sea, son of the local doctor. Completing medical studies at Caius College, and University College Hospital, he returned to his home county to practice. He was house physician to the Norfolk and Norwich Hospital and to the Jenny Lind hospital for 40 years.

He had a passion for nature in the open air and travelled throughout Norfolk in an open car. Dr Long was secretary of the Norfolk and Norwich Naturalists' Society for nearly a quarter of a century, and he was keenly interested in local bird protection societies, which became the forerunners of nature reserves. He had known Scolt Head from boyhood, and he took the initiative in raising a fund to acquire this stretch of sandhills, salt marshes and beaches as a nature reserve. Three years later he realised another ambition - the formation of a Norfolk Trust with powers similar to those of the National Trust, to be run by Norfolk people for the purpose of acquiring and managing nature reserves of its own.

At a luncheon at the George Hotel in Cley he put to a group of friends the idea of a county naturalists trust. It came into being on November 5th 1926. Russell Colman was the first president and Sydney Long was secretary. Out of that has grown the Trust of today, maintaining in its 40 reserves more than 6500 acres of coasts, broads, heath, marshes, fen and woodland. Sydney Long died on July 15th 1939, and his ashes were scattered on Scolt Head.

His diaries are in Norwich Castle Museum, and a Sydney Long Medal has been struck by the Norfolk Naturalists' Trust. "The aim is to honour from time to time those people who make a significant contribution to the conservation of Norfolk wildlife and wild places." (Ted Ellis was the first to receive the medal.)

A wall plaque marks Sydney Long's home in Norwich, in a tall Georgian terrace in Surrey Street. He derived much inspiration from his studies of the work of the very earliest Norfolk naturalists. He once remarked that for him each visit to the heronry at Reedham (no longer there) was like a pilgrimage because grey herons had been described there by Sir Thomas Browne nearly 300 years before.

Herbert de Losinga (1054-1119)

New cathedral

Founder of Norwich Cathedral, Bishop Herbert came to the city in 1094, full of energy and vision. He selected a site close to the river for his new cathedral and the Benedictine monastery which would serve it.

The first Register of Norwich Cathedral Priory tells us that as well as contributing funds of his own, Bishop Herbert decreed "that a certain amount should be contributed from each message in this diocese for the construction of the work of Norwich church." So began the cathedral's first fund-raising campaign. He laid the foundation stone in 1096. The Benedictine monks must have been living in a temporary wooden monastery. He also founded a Benedictine priory on the top of a hill on the other side of the Wensum.

On September 24th 1101, his "Church of Norwich" was finally consecrated. It was not to be completed for many years, but could be used for worship. By the time Bishop Herbert died in 1119 his church was built as far as the twisted pillars. His body was laid before the high altar in a splendid tomb. Both this tomb and its 18th century successor have gone.

Now, a black marble slab set in the floor before the high altar marks his grave. Six iron candlesticks linked with white rope stand guard. A fitting monument for the man who wrote of his church and monastery: "Remember, you enjoy this advantage at my expense, whose toils and labours have won it for you."

He came from a wealthy and well-connected family, and his "life", as far as we know it, started in a Benedictine abbey in Normandy, the abbey of Fecamp, to which he was sent as a young man and of which he eventually became prior. When William the Conqueror died, Herbert threw in his lot with William Rufus, the new King of England, who made him one of his chaplains and brought him to England to be Abbot of Ramsey.

The King looked on the church as a handy source of revenue. When a see fell empty he let it lie vacant for a few years while he drew the revenues. Then he sold it to the highest bidder - and that is believed to be how Herbert de Losinga became Bishop of Thetford in 1091.

Thomas Lovell

Job for life

Thomas Lovell was born in the small parish of Barton Bendish, between Downham Market and Swaffham. He was a Speaker of the House of Commons who became one of the bulwarks of the House of Tudor when the future Henry VII was still a hunted exile. In the first Parliament after the victory at Bosworth Field in 1485 he was made Chancellor of the Exchequer for life. In the struggle to dethrone Henry and put Lambert Simnel in his place, Sir Thomas took the side of the King. When the intrigue ended the King, who had kept Simnel as a lowly servant in the royal kitchen, handed him over to Sir Thomas. He became a falconer in his service.

Jem Mace (1831-1910)

Boxing king

Regarded as the father of modern scientific boxing, Jem Mace was born in Beeston, near East Dereham, son of the village blacksmith. He was apprenticed to a cabinet maker at Wells-next-the-sea on the North Norfolk coast at 15, and frequently boxed at fairs and race meetings before winning national acclaim. He was known as the "Swaffham Gipsy" in those early days, but it is not thought he had any Romany blood.

He won the British heavyweight title in June 1861, stopping the holder, Sam Hurst, in eight rounds. Hurst, who was also champion wrestler of Lancashire, took a severe beating. Mace defended his crown against Tom King the following January. After 43 rounds of fierce fighting, the Norfolk fighter was victorious. King won a return match, and then, after beating American champion John Heenan for the world title decided to retire. Mace took over and became universally known as world champion after beating Joe Goss in 1 hour and 44 minutes. Mace successfully defended his crown against

America-based Tom Allen in Louisiana and American champion Joe Coburn in Mississippi, when the fighters drew over 12 rounds. Mace retired after this contest, but continued to box in exhibitions.

He died in Liverpool at the age of 79. In his later years he was landlord of The Swan in Swan Lane in Norwich. A white stone memorial to Mace, which has been moved around Norwich Cemetery and then lodged for several years in a city stonemason's yard was retrieved and moved to his home village. In April 1976, the memorial was unveiled in Beeston churchyard, outside the church where Jem Mace was christened.

When he was young, Mace played the fiddle "like an angel". His musical wanderings took him to Great Yarmouth when he was 18. He was playing his fiddle in the street to improve his finances when he was accosted by three rough youths. One knocked Jem's beloved instrument from his hand, smashing it. He challenged and defeated two of the youths while the other took to his heels. These battles were watched by an appreciative crowd and a collection was made. One man, subscribing a guinea, remarked that a chap as useful as that with his fists ought to be a prize fighter...

Basil Maine (1894-1972)

Man of music

An outstanding figure in the world of music, locally and nationally, Stephen Basil Maine had many other talents which blossomed in his native Norfolk. He won an organ scholarship to Queen's College, Cambridge, after leaving the City of Norwich School, and went on to win other prizes in reading and essay work during his time at university.

His early life involved many moves, including a spell as assistant organist of Durham Cathedral, and he made a mark as music critic for the Daily Telegraph and the Morning Post. He started writing for the Eastern Daily Press in the mid-1930s when he contributed music reviews on Norwich Triennial Festival events. He also published several books, including "The Life and Works of Edward Elgar", a life-long friend.

He became the Rev Basil Maine in 1940 when at the age of 46 he was ordained in St Edmundsbury Cathedral and took up his first appointment as priest-in-charge of St Andrew's Church in Norwich. After a spell as Rector of Wacton, near Long Stratton, he took appointments in Buckinghamshire and Essex before returning to Norfolk in 1948 to Warham. His last appointment as Vicar of Bramerton and Surlingham began in 1956, and it was from this living that he retired to Cromer in 1958.

As a composer, he wrote a birthday waltz for Princess Margaret and a concert march for the Queen Mother. He also wrote what was known as the Holkham Anthem, entitled "O Holy Spirit Lord of Grace" for special performance at the wedding of Lady Anne Coke, eldest daughter of the Earl of Leicester, to the Hon Colin Tennant in 1956. Basil Maine was radio critic for the Sunday Times and became the first regular music critic of The Spectator magazine. He gave the Bach Commemoration Lecture in Norwich Cathedral in 1950, and his own composition of the Te Deum was given its first public performance during the Colchester Festival of Britain in 1952. During the same event, another of his choral works, "Thou Art My Life", was performed and dedicated to the memory of King George VI.

For several years the president of the Cromer and North Norfolk Festival of Music and Drama, he brought quiet but enthusiastic leadership to one of the county's main events.

George Manby (1765-1854)

Great inventor

George William Manby was born in Denver, in West Norfolk, and went to school in Downham Market. He died at Gorleston in his 90th year and is buried in Hilgay churchyard. He invented the rocket lifesaving apparatus as well as a chemical fire extinguisher, elastic sheets for use at fires, harpoons for whaling, improved types of lifeboats, howitzers and dredgers.

There is an impressive exhibition of his inventions in the Great Yarmouth Maritime Museum. A tablet on the back of his Gorleston house in High Road reads: "In commemoration of the 12th February, 1808, on which day directly eastwards of this site the first life was saved from shipwreck by means of a rope attached to a shot fired from a mortar over the stranded vessel, a method now universally adopted and to which at least 1,000 sailors of various nations owe their lives. 1848."

He often complained about the Government's indifference to his inventions, and thought Queen Victoria should have given him a knighthood. In 1803 he went to London to offer his services to the Secretary of War to assassinate Napoleon. He was refused - and instead he was appointed Barracks Master at Great Yarmouth. It was here that he witnessed a shipwreck involving the loss of 200 lives, a disaster that impelled him to develop his idea of a mortar and rocket apparatus for throwing a line from shore to ship. He came up with the first portable fire extinguisher in 1813 after seeing a blaze in an Edinburgh building where the firemen were unable to get their equipment to the upper floors.

He became a churchwarden at Hilgay, and his name is inscribed, together with that of his fellow churchwarden J Portler, on the church tower, which was built in 1794. There is a tablet in Hilgay Church eulogising his father, Matthew Pepper Manby. It was placed there by George, who described himself as "the last remaining branch of a long line of ancestry and the last of that name."

Mary Mann (1848-1929)

Rural plight

A prolific novelist who published numerous country stories. most of them with Norfolk settings. She lived all her life in the county. Born in Norwich, she became a farmer's wife determined to show rural plight rather than

rustic charm in her stories. The most celebrated, first published in 1902, are "The Fields of Dulditch", containing brutal accounts of the life of labouring families at a time when such poverty was not only commonplace but was seemingly incurable.

These harrowing stories are a considerable challenge to any nostalgic visions we may still harbour about "the good old days" on the land at the turn of the century. Mary Mann settled in the rather isolated village of Shropham - the setting for the Dulditch stories - on marrying in 1871. Her husband farmed 800 acres and assumed the role of caring squire. She helped teach reading at the village school, organised school treats and was a frequent visitor at the labourers' homes. When her husband died in 1913, Mary Mann took a house at Winterton and finally moved to Sheringham. She had one son and three daughters.

Adrian Bell wrote: "The people of Dulditch are more real to me than Hardy's ... although the record of rural penury is so shocking that it awes the writing to simplicity, it leaves an epic quality in the mind, a sort of noble rage which makes for life." D H Lawrence was another ardent admirer of her work. Her one contact with the literary world in London was her nephew, T Fairman Ordish, the Shakespearean scholar who first encouraged her to write and who for some years managed her literary business.

The brutality of labourers to their wives and children is starkly prominent in her depiction of Norfolk village life, and she also dealt with serious problems confronting the farmers. Her first novel, "The Parish of Hilby", includes an episode about a young farmer coping with a strike on his farm, while "Moonlight" opens with the suicide of a bankrupt farmer.

Louis Marchesi (1898-1968)

Round Table

Founder of the international Round Table movement in Norwich in 1927, when about 90 young men gathered together in Suckling House. They agreed it was to be a young men's club; no-one over 40 was to be admitted, and all who reached the age of 40 were to be retired whether they liked it or not.

In fact, the Round Table idea really began two years earlier at a Norwich Rotary Club meeting. When the scheduled speaker failed to arrive, several Rotarians were asked to speak briefly on a "subject you know more about than anyone else in the room". One of those to stand up was Ermino William Louis Marchesi, "pastry cook". He was the eldest son of a Swiss caterer who had settled in England, married an Irish girl and set up business in Norwich.

As Rotarian Marchesi, 27, warmed to his task in addressing older colleagues, he maintained: "What is needed is a club where YOUNG men can get together and exchange their own ideas, not always be fed by older men. They just want to think and work on their own. A club for young men only." So the expression of an idea came forth, and Marchesi was encouraged by the applause and by the dozen or so Rotarians who came up afterwards and agreed with him. Eager discussion took place in the coffee room of Marchesi's restaurant, and on March 14th 1927, the meeting at Suckling House supported the resolution to form a club.

The city's Lord Mayor, Sir Robert Bignold, and the Sheriff, Archie Rice, were both under 40 and backed the idea. Ten years later "Mark", as he became known, was invited to become a national honorary member - he was in for life! By the time Round Table held their 40th anniversary luncheon in 1967, the movement had spread to 28 countries. It was the  founder's last public appearance. He died in December, 1968, and was buried in Norwich beside his wife Dolly.

A memorial service two months later in Westminster Roman Catholic Cathedral was attended by ten of the members who had responded to the call of the young confectioner in 1927. Table No 1 presented to Norwich as a memorial of their famous son a round wooden seat on which shoppers could rest in the shadow of Langford's restaurant (now Moss Bros) where it all began in London Street. The Louis Marchesi public house in Norwich was opened in 1976.

William Marriott

Railway stalwart

William Marriott played a key role in the development of railways in Norfolk. He was engineer and traffic manager for the Midland and Great Northern Joint Railway. In 1921 The Norfolk Chronicle began publishing his memoirs, "Forty Years of a Norfolk Railway" where he recalled the construction of the line from Melton Constable to Sheringham and Cromer .... "There were people in Sheringham who had never seen a locomotive ... old Granny Craske was got into a bath chair and taken to the local crossing to see her first engine. A great deal of work was done by us in the early development of Sheringham. The directors set up the first building estate, built waterworks, laid the main drain, got hotel and gasworks built and gave the place its start in life." His name is perpetuated in the new settlement of Thorpe Marriott on the outskirts of Norwich. The railway line used to run through the middle of the developed site.

Frederick Marryat (1792-1848)

Langham period

Ill health meant an early retirement from the Navy for Captain Frederick Marryat after a colourful career, and he bought an estate of 1000 acres at Langham in North Norfolk in 1830. He had been made a Companion of the Order of the Bath for his services in the Burma campaign, and he invented an improved method of signalling for ships. For this he was elected a Fellow of the Royal Society. He did not move to Langham until 1843, leasing Manor Cottage and the farmland to a succession of tenants while he lived in Wimbledon and Brighton.

Eventually, the old sea rover turned Norfolk farmer and also began writing the seven novels which belong to the Langham period, including "Children of the New Forest". Marryat seems to have been a popular landlord and local magistrate, although he was far too rash and extravagant to make a success of farming. One of his schemes was to drain the salt marshes around Cley. He appointed the most notorious poacher in the district, William Barnes, as his gamekeeper. Charles Dickens paid Captain Marryat a visit at Manor Cottage.

Towards the end of 1847, Marryat left Langham for Hastings and Brighton in an effort to improve his health. He returned to Norfolk following news of the loss of his sailor son Frederick on *HMS Avenger*. The shock proved fatal. Captain Marryat had four sons and seven daughters, but only one son, Frank, survived him - and he died at the age of 28.

Captain Marryat was buried in Langham churchyard, south-west of the tower. The men of the estate carried his coffin to his grave.

The Langham village sign, carved by Harry Carter of Swaffham in 1979, includes a ship to represent the Marryat connection.

Robert Marsham (1708-1797)

Tree planter

Naturalist and writer Robert Marsham was a Norfolk squire with a passion for trees. Some of those which Marsham grew from seed in his own nursery are still flourishing, and those of his planting on the edge of a large heath running towards Norwich can still be appreciated along the boundary between Stratton Strawless and Horsford.

In 1780 his work on the recording of growth in trees earned him a Fellowship of the Royal Society, a reward which by no means persuaded him that his practical work was over ... for at 85 he set out once more on the planting of a new wood. Next to planting trees, his great delights were pruning and thinning. He loved to try new and unorthodox methods of pruning and pollarding his trees, and new devices for promoting their growth, especially by digging frequently and extensively around the roots. In two communications to the Royal Society he described his experiments to increase the growth of trees by washing and rubbing their trunks.

The squire of Stratton Strawless was quite an influential character. He corresponded with Gilbert White, the naturalist of Selborne, and was also a friend of William Windham, of Felbrigg, and William's tutor, Benjamin Stillingfleet. They had many interests in common, and the study of botany and of natural history in particular. Marsham also taught landscape gardener Humphrey Repton while he lived at Sustead.

It was as early as 1736 that Marsham had started to compile annual tables of what he called the "Indications of Spring". He noted the earliest snowdrop, brimstone butterfly and swallow, the earliest singing of thrush and cuckoo and nightingale, the dates when a variety of trees came into leaf, the first time he heard frogs croaking or saw rooks building their nests - in all, 26 of the most familiar occurrences of every spring. He kept these tables without a break from 1736 until the year of his death, a span of 60 years. He continued to plant and to experiment with trees until the very end of his life in his 90th year. No man can outlive the trees he has planted.

Sarah Martin (1791-1843)

A warm heart

A woman with a warm heart and a dauntless spirit, Sarah Martin was born in Caister-on-sea, near Great Yarmouth. At the age of 19 she began visits to the workhouse where she chatted and read to the sick and aged inmates. She also instructed the workhouse children in the Scriptures.

When she decided to take her philanthropic work to prisoners in jail, it must have taken considerable courage to persevere. She first gained admittance in 1819. Then she bought material for women's clothes and showed prisoners how to make them up in an attempt to beat boredom and idleness. Although extremely grateful for any gift from the prisoners, she was most scrupulous about receiving money on her own behalf. Yarmouth Town Council had great difficulty in persuading her, poor though she was, to accept the sum of 12 pounds a year.

When prisoners were released she helped in every way possible and even had a fund from which she could help those she thought deserving of extra support. Strain and hardships of the past began to tell in the spring of 1843. She died in the October and was buried in Caister churchyard near her grandmother.

She gave more than she had, and did her best to blot out the shameful scenes which made the Old Tollhouse at Yarmouth a scandal to the town. It was a bishop who, in giving a donation to a Sarah Martin memorial window, said: "I would canonise Sarah Martin if I could."

Her parents died when she was quite young and she was brought up by her grandmother, Mrs Bonnet, a glovemaker who lived in a small thatched cottage in Beach Road, Caister. When she was 14, Sarah was apprenticed to a dressmaker and soon acquired the skills to set up by herself. She went on to become one of the most important prison reformers of the 19th century - but even today her work does not receive the full recognition it deserves.

Harriet Martineau (1802-1876)

Lucid thinker

A prolific writer, Harriet Martineau not only shone in the spheres of literature and politics, but scored personal triumphs over physical disabilities, poverty and misfortune. Born without the sensations of taste and smell, and deaf by the time she was 18, she had a sad childhood. She wrote in later years: "My life has had no spring."

Born in Norwich the sixth of eight children, she was raised in a stern and resolutely pious atmosphere. Her hopes of becoming a teacher were shattered by increasing deafness, and so she turned to writing. Her mother felt she would be better employed in sewing, but Harriet began to write anonymously for the Monthly Repository, a Unitarian periodical. In 1826 her father's business crashed and the shock killed him. Harriet had become engaged, but her fiance died from a brain

illness. Now acutely aware of the inequalities and miseries of her fellows she began her lifelong study of social reform and political economy. Her first book, "Illustrations of Political Economy", was published with the help of Charles Fox and brought immediate success. Her future assured, Harriet moved to London in 1832 and met all the literary celebrities of the day.

She went to America a couple of years later and her progressive mind found a new challenge in the slave question. She became a keen supporter of the Abolitionist party and the article published on her return to Britain, in the Westminster Review, introduced English readers to what she called "The Martyr Age in the United States". Struck down by a mystery complaint, Harriet had to spend five years indoors until she was cured by mesmerism. Even during her confinement she kept up her literary output, writing a novel, four children's stories and many articles. She became the first woman journalist to join a big London daily when she became leader writer of the Daily News in 1852. Her closing years were spent at Ambleside in the Lake District.

A lucid thinker and a fearless champion of any cause she pursued, Harriet suffered almost continuously from poor health, but never became the victim of self-pity. She said there was nothing remarkable about her life: "In short, I can popularise while I can neither discover nor invent."

Nugent Monck (1878-1958)

Maddermarket man

The son of a Shropshire clergyman, Nugent Monck founded the famous Maddermarket Theatre in Norwich in 1921. A former Roman Catholic chapel, which had been used as a warehouse and Salvation Army citadel at the turn of the century, was transformed into a delightful Elizabethan theatre. It cost £3,300 raised from supporters, and Norwich took happily to it.

The production, settings and costumes were of a high standard, and the actors were then, as now, anonymous. The theatre built up an international reputation and Monck's reign at the Maddermarket lasted until his retirement in 1952. He produced all of Shakespeare's plays between 1921 and 1932, but for all his devotion to the Bard he was not above cutting out whole scenes and inventing linking passages of his own. He was a martinet on stage, accustomed to giving orders and having them obeyed without question. He once said: "Anyone who wants to act for me must bring unquestioning obedience and his own greasepaint."

There were many invitations to Monck and his Norwich Players to tour abroad. His response was emphatic: "We stay here in our own theatre and if people want to see us badly enough they can make the pilgrimage. The men and women of the Maddermarket have other jobs during the day, and certainly cannot go gallivanting about the world for this whimsey or that." He did lecture for the British Council in Germany and the West Indies. In 1950 he produced "The Merchant of Venice" in Kingston, Jamaica. He was awarded the Order of the British Empire in 1946, and was made a Commander of the British Empire shortly before his death.

It was after successfully producing a pageant in the city in 1909 that he decided to settle in Norwich. The Norwich Players were formed with the Music House (now Wensum Lodge) in King Street as their first home. A decade later came the chance to look to a long term future from a permanent base at the Maddermarket Theatre.

It continues to provide excellent fare for drama-lovers, with a plaque outside saluting the vision and energy of Nugent Monck. His character was once summed up as "an extraordinary mixture of Celtic temperament and Puritan upbringing."

Alicia Meynell

Racing exploits

Alicia Meynell, daughter of a Norwich watchmaker, is regarded as the first woman jockey in the British Isles. The Racing Calendar honoured her exploits under the name of "Mrs T". She made her debut when she was 22 before a big crowd at York races in 1804. She rode Col. Thomas Thornton's *Vingaretta* in a match for 500 guineas and 1000 guineas over a distance of four miles against Mr Flint Brown's *Thornville*, ridden by the owner. Alicia made the running for a good three miles, but her horse tired and Thornton won easily. The game Norwich-born rider was in the saddle a year later at

York, and racing against her this time was a famous jockey of the day, Francis Buckle. "Mrs T" made the pace from start to finish and won by half a neck. A reporter wrote: "Her bold and excellent jockeyship elicited the admiration of the assembled thousands who hailed her success with the most enthusiastic shouts and applause and congratulations."

Ralph Mottram (1883-1971)

Literary doyen

For many years the literary doyen of Norwich, R H Mottram was born in the city, of which he became Lord Mayor, and educated there and in Lausanne. He started work as a clerk in a local bank, and in 1904 met the writer John Galsworthy, who encouraged his literary ambitions.

He served in France from 1914 until 1919 and in 1924 published "The Spanish Farm", filmed as "Roses of

Picardy". His first novel, it won the Hawthornden Prize and featured a preface written by Galsworthy. Its sequels, "Sixty-Four, Ninety-Four!" and "The Crime of Vanderlynden's" were equally successful and in 1927 the three were published as The Spanish Farm Trilogy.

In all, Mottram wrote about 60 books, with many of his later novels set in East Anglia. Generally regarded as the best of the local books "Our Mr Dormer" is based on Gurney's Bank (later Barclays) where the author served for several years. Three generations of Dormers serve "Doughty's Bank" as chief clerk. Mottram's knowledge of his home city was unrivalled, and his biography of his father, "Portrait of an Unknown Victorian", and autobiographical books complete his original picture of middle-class life in a provincial capital city.

In 1966 Mottram was awarded the honorary degree of Doctor of Letters by the University of East Anglia. When he died in 1971 his friend Eric Fowler (Jonathan Mardle of the Eastern Daily Press) said in his tribute: "He was a lively connection with the Victorians about whom he loved to write and talk; and he was an example of their finest virtues, which were loyalty and faithfulness. He recognised the defects as well as the virtues of the past and kept to the end of his life the Victorian faith in progress. It feels as if a whole chapter of the history of Norwich, and indeed of England, has gone with him. Nobody else in this city will ever know or express quite so much as he did about the spirit of the place."

Alfred Munnings (1878-1959)

Colourful artist

The region's most famous painter of this century, Alfred James Munnings was the son of a miller - like Constable - and grew up at Mendham Mill on the Norfolk-Suffolk border.

The scenery of the Waveney Valley was his earliest love. He moved to Norwich at 14 to train as a poster designer and studied each evening at the Norwich School of Art. The first of his 289 pictures to be hung

by the Royal Academy was accepted for the summer exhibition of 1898. Munnings is best known for his paintings of horses, and to the end of his days he remained an enraptured recorder of sales, fairs, hunts and races.

He found both fame and notoriety. In 1928 a retrospective exhibition of his work at the Norwich Castle Museum attracted 86,000 visitors in six weeks. But while he longed to be free to paint East Anglian scenes he had to accept numerous commissions for equestrian portraits to pay the bills. He was elected president of the Royal Academy in 1944 and was knighted. He took full advantage of his elevated status to attack modern art, agreeing with Winston Churchill that the punishment he would like to mete out to Picasso would be to kick his backside.

It was hardly surprising that this complex and rumbustious man should become caricatured as a blimpish bigot, and so much of the inventiveness of his best work became obscured.

A regular visitor to Newmarket, he had a studio in the town during the 1950s. His favourite subject showed horses and jockeys lined up and raring to go at the starting line. One such picture smashed the auction record for the artist when it was sold by Sotheby's of New York in 1987. "The Start at Newmarket; Study No 4" fetched a hammer price of 1.1 million dollars.

Munnings, who became a Freeman of the City of Norwich, underlined his writing talents in his three autobiographical works, and he also wrote ballads of a rollicking and rather coarse variety. He put them over with great fervour and was also a wonderful storyteller. His ashes lie in St Paul's Cathedral, where his memorial tablet, next to that of John Constable, bears these words:

O Friend, how very lovely are the things
The English things you helped us to perceive!

Christopher Myngs (1625-1666)

The other Victory

Sir Christopher lived through the period of the English Civil War, the Commonwealth and the Restoration. Baptised at Salthouse, he was the first of that trio of North Norfolk admirals, each of whom played an important part in the navy of the day - the other two being Sir John Narborough and Sir Cloudesley Shovel.

Samuel Pepys makes several references to Myngs in his diary. He saw several years of service in West Indian waters, and was promoted to vice-admiral in 1664. He hoisted his flag in the *Royal Oak,* this ship being part of the Channel squadron under the overall command of Prince Rupert. In June 1665, Myngs took part in the battle of Lowestoft, the opening battle of the second Dutch War. The battle ended in a decisive victory for the English, and Myngs was knighted for his services. He then took command of a

squadron guarding the Channel trade routes and his work was commended on several occasions.

In April 1666, he hoisted the flag in the *Victory*, and so became the first Norfolk admiral to be connected with a ship of that name. (Not, of course, the same ship - Nelson's *Victory* was launched in 1765). During the first four days of June in 1666, the Dutch and English fleets fought one of the longest and toughest battles in history. The English suffered a heavy defeat, losing 17 ships and 8000 men. This defeat was to be reversed only a few weeks later at the Battle of Orfordness, but Myngs did not live to see it.

The *Victory* did not take part in the first three days of fighting in what is now called the Four Days' Battle. When Myngs did get involved he was shot through the throat. He held the lips of the wound together with his fingers. Another bullet passed through his neck - and so he became the first of two British admirals of Norfolk extraction to be shot and mortally wounded aboard a ship called the *Victory*.

John Narborough (1640-1688)

Leading seaman

Narborough was baptised in Cockthorpe Church and went to sea at an early age, possibly with Admiral Myngs from nearby Salthouse. Narborough was involved in the Battle of Sole Bay off Southwold in 1672. He was promoted to rear-admiral and knighted the following year. After distinguished Mediterranean service he was posted to the West Indies where he caught a fever and died. He was buried at sea, minus his bowels and other internal organs which were pickled and brought home for burial.

Horatio Nelson (1758-1805)

Favourite son

Norfolk's favourite son went to sea at 12 years of age and became the most brilliant and most honoured naval leader Britain has known. His father was rector of Burnham Thorpe. His mother was the daughter of Dr

Maurice Suckling, Prebendary of Westminster. Nelson's maternal great-grandmother was sister to Sir Robert Walpole, statesman and first minister to the Georges.

Nelson went to three Norfolk schools; a statue in the Cathedral Close in Norwich commemorates his time there. He also went to school in Downham Market and to Paston in North Walsham. It was during his time at Paston that young Nelson went into the headmaster's garden at night to gather pears for his friends. "I only took them," he is recorded as saying, "because every other boy was afraid." He went to sea at 12 despite obvious physical weaknesses, and the "glow of patriotism" kindled within him was to burn so brightly during a glittering career.

He was particularly dear to the people of Great Yarmouth, and when he stepped ashore in November, 1800, after the Battle of the Nile, he was given a tumultuous reception and carried in triumph to the Wrestler's Hotel. There he was presented with the freedom of the borough. It is said that the town clerk, when about to administer the oath, and noting that Nelson's left hand was placed on the Bible, exclaimed: "Your right hand, my lord." "That" Nelson replied laconically, "is at Tenerife".

When All Saints Church at Burnham Thorpe was restored, the Admiralty, in 1881, presented, among other relics, wood from his ship *Victory* for the lectern and rood cross. The bust of Nelson in the chancel was given by the London Society of East Anglians.

There are many other monuments and souvenirs associated with Nelson. Yarmouth perpetuated him in the famous Nelson Column on the south denes. The crowning figure of Britannia, 144 feet above the harbour, gazes westward across the Norfolk countryside. No doubt Nelson would have turned away from the sea

had he lived to an old age instead of dying in another hour of triumph at Trafalgar.

Amelia Opie (1771-1853)

Gay Quaker

Novelist and poet, Amelia Opie allied wit, wisdom and gaiety of mind with the sturdy piety of the Quakers. She was known as "The Gay Quaker", and Opie Street, which runs between Castle Meadow and London Street in Norwich, was laid out on the site of the last house she lived in.

She made an early entrance into local society, and at 18 wrote a tragedy called "Adelaide" which was privately produced in Norwich with Amelia in the leading role. She also developed a keen interest in social problems, and seems to have been fascinated by the psychology of crime, attending trials at all the Norwich assizes. She moved into London society to become acquainted with leading artistic and literary lights of the day. A friendship with the actress Mrs Siddons lasted for the rest of her life.

Amelia married painter John Opie in 1798 and her writing career flourished. John died in 1807 and his widow shared her time between Norwich and London. Then the serious side of her character underwent a certain change, and she began attending Quaker services. The popular idea of a Quaker in her day was of someone who took no part in frivolity of any kind, but nothing could dampen this vivacious woman's zest for enjoyment.

She did give up writing novels and took to visiting workhouses and prisons instead. She did adopt the Quaker mode of dress, but managed to brighten its plain style and drab colouring by having hers made of the finest silks and satins. One of her chief interests was the

Anti-Slavery Society and she attended a convention in London in 1840 as delegate for Norwich.

When she was nearly 80 she bought the house on Castle Meadow where Opie Street stands today. But far from living the normal life of an old lady, she insisted upon indulging in her favourite occupation of attending the assizes. And in 1851, when dear Amelia was 82, she went to the Great Exhibition in London. She was in her wheeled chair - and challenged another old lady, in a similar vehicle, to a race round the grounds. If the contest did not take place it was not due to any unwillingness on the part of the ebullient Mrs Opie!

James Paget (1814-1899)

Royal surgeon

A leading surgeon and medical authority in his day, James Paget was born in Great Yarmouth, the youngest of nine surviving children of 17 born to his parents Samuel and Betsy. The family had been in the town for 200 years, and Samuel was a prosperous merchant and brewer. He became mayor in 1817, but his business declined and he sold up.

James was apprenticed to a local surgeon in 1830, and then moved on to St Bartholomew's Hospital in London as a student and won every single prize in his first year. He became curator of the hospital museum and then warden of the residential college for medical students. A feature of these first ten years was his poverty and the hard work he put into his studies.

In 1844 he married Lydia North after being engaged for eight years. Three years later he was appointed an assistant surgeon and lecturer at Bart's. His success began when he set up in private practice in Henrietta Street. In 1858 he moved to 1 Harewood Place, where he spent the rest of his life. He left Bart's after 37 years there, and his portrait by John Millais still hangs in the hospital. He was made a baronet and appointed Surgeon Extraordinary to The Queen and Surgeon in Ordinary to the Prince of Wales.

He gave up operating in 1878 but was still lecturing at the age of 80. He was a brilliant speaker who never used notes; he always memorised his talks. He was President of the International Medical Congress in 1881. When he died in 1899 a funeral service was held in Westminster Abbey. He gave his name to Paget's Disease, of which there are seven forms, the best known being those of the breast and the bones. In 1984 the Yarmouth District General Hospital was renamed the James Paget Hospital. One of his favourite sayings was: "No man ever did good work who was not frequently overworked."

Thomas Paine (1737-1809)

Political giant

No political writer made a more immediate impact on his own time than Thetford-born Thomas Paine. His pamphlet "Common Sense" crystallised the arguments for independence which fuelled the American Revolution. His "Rights of Man", written in defence of the French Revolution, made him the spokesman for English radicalism against the oppressive tradition of the 18th century. It sold 200,000 copies and it caused Paine to be tried for seditious libel and his effigy to be hanged, shot and burned.

His "Age of Reason" was the first book to come out and say in plain English that the Bible was irrational and inconsistent, and that it was not the voice of God. Paine dealt with the big issues and took it for granted that they were everybody's to consider.

He died in poverty in New York in 1809. He had to wait until 1945 to be elected to the American Hall of Fame to stand with George Washington and Paul Revere.

Paine's father, a Quaker, kept a shop in Thetford as a staymaker, in modern terms a maker of women's corsets. He also ran a small farm and made enough money to be able to send his son to the local grammar school from the age of six until he was 14. He had a scientific bent and had the chance to pursue these interests on moving to London. He attended "philosophical lectures", but after his marriage settled for the role of customs officer. He sailed for Philadelphia in America in 1774.

Before a statue of Paine was erected in Thetford in 1964, there had been only a bronze plaque paid for by American airmen who had been stationed near Thetford in the Second World War. The statue was sculpted by Sir Charles Wheeler, at one time President of the Royal Academy. Tom Paine has a quill pen in his right hand and in his left a copy of "Rights of Man".

The political dispute over the erection of the statue led to the founding of The Thomas Paine Society, of which Michael Foot became the president. While the 200th anniversary of Paine's birth had achieved little more than a dinner in the Guildhall in London, the Society saw to it that the 250th anniversary in 1987 was widely acclaimed.

Matthew Parker (1504-1575)

The middle way

Born in Norwich, where he attended the grammar school, Matthew Parker became Archbishop of Canterbury when Elizabeth I came to the throne. He is remembered mostly for the moderation with which he sought to mediate between Puritans and Roman Catholics and establish the Church of England as a middle way between them.

It was while he was reading for his degree at Corpus Christi College in Cambridge that he was converted to Protestantism and came to the notice of Henry VIII, who made him chaplain to Anne Boleyn. On the eve of her execution in 1536 Anne placed her infant daughter, the future Queen Elizabeth, in his charge. Elizabeth would remember this when she ascended the throne.

Parker was in Norwich with his family during Kett's Rebellion. He did not lack courage for he went to Mousehold Heath to preach to Kett and his 20,000 men and urged them to lay down their arms and return home. Parker was threatened with pikes and arrows and had to beat a hasty retreat.

He also lives by a famous remark of the Virgin Queen, not to him but to his wife. Having been magnificently entertained at Lambeth Palace, Elizabeth, who respected the Archbishop but disapproved of married clergy, took leave of poor Madam Parker with the splendid equivocation: "Madam I may not call you; Mistress I am ashamed to call you; but yet I thank you."

One of his first tasks as Archbishop of Canterbury was to have a new translation made of the Bible and he appointed a Committee to do this. A copy of this "Bishop's Bible" is in St Peter Hungate Church museum in the city. His biggest success was the Elizabethan religious settlement with the publication of his 39 Articles. These statements of religious principles were required to be accepted by every practising clergyman.

Norwich and its grammar school produced another Archbishop of Canterbury. Thomas Tenison (1636-

1715) rose high in the favour of William and Mary after the Glorious Revolution of 1688, and was appointed Archbishop of Canterbury in 1694. One of his last acts was to crown George I.

Margaret Paston (1421-1484)

Woman of letters

A formidable woman who stands out in the history of 15th century Norfolk, Margaret Mauteby was born in Reedham, near Great Yarmouth. She inherited her father's estates and married John Paston in 1440. Judge William Paston, John's father, had elevated the family to the rank of country gentry and had bought up lordships and property in different parts of Norfolk. To his son and heir, John, fell the task of holding on to the family estates in a lawless and rapacious age. It was a task which had to be shared by Margaret.

John Paston, a lawyer, spent much time in London, and became a trusted friend of Sir John Fastolf, who made him the main heir to his extensive property. That property was to bring so much trouble to the Pastons. In the frequent absence of husband and sons, Margaret acted as estate and household manager, ordering provisions, fuel and animal fodder and supervising the buying and selling of horses and so on.

It was during the major crises in her husband's life that Margaret showed her real mettle. As early as 1449 she had been left to defend the manor house at Gresham and was carried out bodily as she and the servants were outnumbered by invaders. She had plenty of experience by the time she had to organise the defence of Caister Castle and the manors of Hellesdon and Drayton.

No side of the complicated legal and territorial struggles which surrounded the Pastons for so long was too difficult for the redoubtable Margaret to understand and deal with. She survived her husband by 18 years and was buried at Mautby, near Yarmouth, when she died in November 1484.

A high proportion of the famous Paston Letters were written to or for her. These letters give an intimate picture of everyday life in the 15th century ... a family saga of rifts and reconciliations, births, elopements, marriages and deaths. They also portray a family on the fringe of great events, especially as England is divided by the Wars of the Roses. The earliest great collection of family letters in English, they span three generations of the family who took their name from the village where they lived near the north-east coast of Norfolk.

Arthur Patterson (1857-1935)

Breydon champion

Arthur Henry Patterson was a self-taught naturalist who became an authority on Breydon Water, the estuary at Great Yarmouth which inspired much of his writing under the name "John Knowlittle".

Born in a Yarmouth Row, the son of a shoemaker, his first regular job was as a truant officer; before that he had been a relief postman, warehouseman, pedlar, salesman, zookeeper and showman. But it was as a naturalist and writer that he excelled. He wrote 26 books along with hundreds of articles for newspapers, periodicals, leaflets and reports for natural history organisations. "Wild Fowlers and Poachers", his book published in 1929, was "my last testament of Breydon - those I knew as a lad - eelers, smelters, walking gunmen, wild fowlers, poachers." It was typed at his dictation by a young disciple called Ted Ellis, himself destined to become another outstanding Norfolk naturalist.

Yarmouth honoured Patterson in 1957 when they unveiled a tablet in George Street close to where he was born a century earlier. In May 1935, just a few months before his death, he was elected an Associate of the Linnean Society of London. Recognition at last! Congratulations flooded in, including a letter from the

Duchess of Bedford, who had put his name forward in 1906. She wrote: "It is rather a pity they wait quite so long to give these awards as they would be more appreciated when one is a little younger."

In his old age Patterson still lauded Breydon Water for the "salt tides and a great green level outlook, not to mention solitude." He wrote: "The question has often been put to me, 'What can we do with Breydon?' My invariable answer has been, 'Let it alone'".

He haunted Breydon at all hours, learning by observation. It is doubtful whether he ever earned more than 30 shillings a week; he once said he "enjoyed the hobby of a gentleman on the screw of a jackass." He wrote for the local papers under the typically self-effacing name of "John Knowlittle". Ted Ellis said of his old hero: "He looked about like a Sir Thomas Browne, seeking new wonders and delving into mysteries with the eagerness of a child of the Renaissance. He had many young disciples who sought guidance from near and far - and how generous he was in encouraging them!"

Fermor and John Pepys

Samuel's cousins

Norfolk cousins of the famous diarist Samuel Pepys, Fermor and John Pepys are buried in Mileham church. Fermor in particular was held in high regard if his epitaph is anything to go by: "He lived a Christian, died a believer, and lives a saint." He died in 1660, two years after his brother.

Samuel Peto (1809-1889)

Rail pioneer

Sir Samuel Morton Peto, the Victorian rail pioneer, took his rightful place in Norfolk history in November 1989, a century after his death. After months of fundraising a bust of the famous builder by sculptor Jack Pooley was unveiled at Norwich Thorpe railway station by his great-grandson Sir Henry Peto.

Sir Samuel was a major railway contractor, MP for Norwich and a prominent Baptist. Although the Thorpe station built by him was replaced in the 1880s by the present station, its twin survives in Rosario, Argentina, where Peto later used the plans for a railway he was building there. The Great Yarmouth - Norwich Railway completed in 1844 was Norfolk's first, and Norwich was connected to London only 14 months later. His system of paying navvies regularly, making sure they were well fed and attended school and chapel in their free time rather than the pub was the key to his success.

Peto extended his personal interest in the area by buying the little-used navigation from Norwich to Lowestoft and building a line alongside it. He also purchased Somerleyton Hall from which to control his East Anglian assets. The crowning touch was to be elected MP for Norwich just five years after starting the railway.

Peto's cousin, Thomas Grissell, was his fellow-contractor for that first line in Norfolk. They had inherited an uncle's building firm some years before, and had already done much railway work in the Midlands. They were also active in the transformation of the West End of London.

The opening of Norfolk's first line was celebrated in style. A train of 14 vehicles was assembled behind one of the little engines, which took 50 minutes for the journey to Yarmouth. It returned later that day to Norwich in 44 minutes - not far short of the present journey time. The Assembly Rooms in Norwich were decked out for the occasion and Peto presided over a lengthy banquet with many toasts. The following day a similar event took place in Yarmouth.

Fuller Pilch (1804-1870)

Master batsman

The top batsman in England for well over a decade was born in Horningtoft, near Fakenham. He was lured away from the Norfolk cricket scene to Kent in 1836 by an offer of £100 per year. Fuller Pilch played until he was 51, and played a major part in again making Kent a force in the game.

Haygarth, writing in 1862, described Pilch as "the best batsman that has yet appeared. His style of batting was very commanding, extremely forward, and he seemed to crush the best bowling by his long forward plunge just before it had time to shoot, or rise, or do mischief by catches." The Earl of Bessborough, who had played cricket with him, wrote: "I always put Pilch and Grace in a class by themselves, and I put them very much on a level."

While he was with Norfolk, for whom his brothers Nathaniel and William also played, Pilch scored emphatic victories over Yorkshireman Tom Marsden, the single wicket champion. Pilch won by an innings and 70 runs in Norwich and by 127 runs in Sheffield. In 1834, before Pilch went to Kent, Norfolk beat Yorkshire in what was probably the first county match to be played in Norwich. Pilch made 87 not out and 73. The next year Pilch again distinguished himself against Yorkshire, scoring 157 not out in Norfolk's second innings.

When Pilch was lured away by Kent he took with him another useful Norfolk cricketer in William Stearman of Aldborough, whose batting won him a place in the Kent side from 1836 to 1840.

In retirement, Fuller Pilch kept the Saracen's Head public house in Canterbury, and is reputed to have refused all appeals for credit as he did for leg before wicket when umpiring, scornfully crying: "Bowl 'em out!". One of the colourful legends which was told about Fuller Pilch is that he carried a scythe around with his cricket gear to mow the outfield before the match began.

His name appeared for the first time in the Norfolk team which played against MCC at Lord's in 1820. The game is remembered not for Pilch's display - he scored 0 and 2 - but for the first recorded double century, in cricket. William Ward made 278 for MCC. However, Pilch was soon to prove himself the best of an era.

Richard Porson (1759-1808)

Leading scholar

Born on Christmas Day 1759 at East Ruston, near North Walsham, Richard Porson became the greatest classicist of his time. He went to the village schools at Bacton and Happisburgh. At Happisburgh the master, Mr Summers, taught him Latin and Maths, and his father made him repeat the day's lessons each evening.

The Rev T Hewitt, curate of East Ruston, took him into his own house when he was eleven and educated him with his own children. Porson went to Eton from 1774 to 1778 and then moved on to Trinity College, Cambridge, to embark on a remarkable career. He became Regius Professor of Greek at Cambridge and went on to edit definitive editions of many Greek plays.

Porson, who became addicted to alcohol and died at 48, had a prodigious memory. At school he had no trouble repeating a lesson he had learned 12 months earlier. He didn't make a single mistake - and had not seen the book in the meantime. At Eton he would produce Horace from memory, and later in life he could repeat Smollett's "Roderick Random" from beginning to end. He once entertained a company at a friend's house by giving a translation of an Italian novel he had sat up all night to read!

He wrote many humorous verses, including this one:

I went to Strasburg, where I got drunk
With that most learn'd Professor Brunk:
I went to Wortz, where I got drunken
With that more learn'd Professor Ruhnken.

His humour and wit could leave rivals floundering. He was once arguing with an acquaintance who, getting the worst of it, said: "Professor, my opinion of you is most contemptible." "Sir" replied Porson, "I never knew an opinion of yours that was not contemptible."

And on being told that Dr Pretyman, the Bishop of Lincoln, had been left a large estate by a person who had seen him only once, he said: "It would not have happened if the person had seen him twice."

Lincoln Ralphs (1909-1978)

Education chief

Chief education officer for Norfolk from 1950 to 1974, Sir Lincoln Ralphs often provoked controversy with his views - but remarkable progress was made in many areas during his time at the helm. Chairman of the National Schools Council from 1972 to 1975, he was knighted for his services to education in 1973.

Born in Shropshire, he spent much of his early life in Yorkshire. He had a brilliant career at the University of Sheffield, becoming a Master of Science, a Bachelor of Law and receiving his doctorate for research carried out in South Yorkshire schools.

During his years as Norfolk's chief education officer, 34 secondary modern schools and one grammar school - at Thorpe - were built in the county. Norfolk College of Arts and Technology at King's Lynn was largely his inspiration and he was the main force behind the creation of Easton School of Agriculture. He was closely involved in the founding of the University of East Anglia, and even more with the development of Wymondham College as the largest co-educational boarding school in Europe.

The issue that caused most controversy in his latter years was the question of comprehensive education in Norfolk. He often clashed with those who wanted to move faster towards the introduction of the new system. He was most concerned with local determination and expressed his passionate concern for the individual child in the education system.

Sir Lincoln's interest in religious education was reflected in his presidency of the National Sunday School Union, and he was also the first Methodist layman to preach in Norwich Cathedral. Among the honours he received were honorary degrees from the Universities of Surrey and Lancaster and the Fellowship of the College of Preceptors. Sir Lincoln was involved in a great number of organisations at local and national level, among them being the Schools Council, an independent advisory body supported by the Department of Education and local authorities.

Arthur Ransome (1884-1967)

Classic stories

Arthur Ransome fired the imagination of generations of children, and set some of his classic stories on the Norfolk Broads. He published "Swallows and Amazons" in 1930 after settling in the Lake District and visited the Broads for the first time the following year. A series of a dozen children's novels gloried in sailing holidays and exploring.

Ransome saw immediately that the Broads were at the crossroads; the day of the wherry had gone and the age of the motor cruiser was in the ascendent, bringing in its wake all sorts of pollution. "Coot Club" gave an accurate picture of the pressures piling up on Broadland's fragile ecology, all seen through the eyes of childhood. Ransome's books have inspired countless holidays on the Broads and helped teach respect for the beauties available.

He went to Russia in 1913 to escape an unhappy first marriage and aimed to collect fairy stories for translation. But he got caught up in the march of history, remaining in the country during the Great War as a correspondent for the Daily News. One of the cables he sent to London broke the news of Rasputin's death. He became a special correspondent for the Manchester Guardian during the Russian Revolution, gaining the trust of the Bolshevik leaders who admired his impartiality. He played chess with Lenin and eventually married Trotsky's secretary. He emerged from his Russian experience with a need to get away from it all - and "Swallows and Amazons" set him on the path to fame as a children's author.

The Ransomes were an East Anglian family and Arthur traced his Quaker ancestors as far as a Norwich miller in the 16th century. Arthur's great-great-grandfather left the area and became a well-known Manchester surgeon, but his brother remained to start the Ipswich firm of Ransome and Rapier.

A Ransome weekend, to celebrate the author's life was staged on Ranworth Broad at the end of September in 1990 as part of the Norfolk and Norwich Festival. There were exhibitions, talks, film shows and a coach trip round the Broads. Boaters, blazers and wicker picnic baskets bobbed in boats on the Broads as 1200 people paid tribute to Ransome.

Humphrey Repton (1752-1818)

Landscape star

Most of the great landscape designers of the 18th century worked in Norfolk, and Humphrey Repton made a significant contribution. His views on the arrangement and improvement of landscape were mainly derived from those of "Capability" Brown, who died in 1783. Repton saw himself as his successor - and was regarded as such by his contemporaries.

Born in Bury St Edmund's, he lived in Norwich and then at Old Hall, Sustead, in the early years of his life. Although he took to landscaping at the relatively late age of 39 he soon built up a large following and worked on at least 16 estates in Norfolk. It was said that because he loved the county so much he charged local owners less than his normal fees. He worked on large parks at Blickling and Holkham, but also found time for relatively small projects at Northrepps, Honing, Hoveton St John and Bracondale.

As a competent water-colourist he developed the technique of writing and illustrating a "Red Book" for each estate which summarised his proposals. Sheringham Hall is the best surviving example of Repton's work and was own favourite. He converted an area of wood and farmland into a park of unparalleled beauty. Much of the woodland was already mature but Repton thickened and extended it, for example by planting newly imported types of rhododendron.

He is buried in Aylsham Church; his tomb reads:

"The tomb of Humphrey Repton,
*   who died March 24,1818.*
Not like the Egyptian tyrants - consecrate,
Unmixt with others, shall my dust remain:
But mould'ring, blended, melting into earth,
Mine shall give form and colour to the rose;
And while its vivid blossoms cheer mankind,
Its perfumed odour shall ascend to heaven."

Edward Rigby (1747-1822)

Medical pioneer

Rigby was a surgeon and apothecary who studied medicine in Norwich and was associated with the founding of the Norfolk and Norwich Hospital when he was only 24. He became an expert at operating to remove gallstones, introduced vaccination into the city and also ran a smallpox hospital.

Amy Robsart (1532-1560)

Did she fall?

Mystery still surrounds the name of this 16th century Norfolk girl who may indirectly have had a great influence on the monarchs and dynasties who ruled England.

Amy was brought up on her father's various estates, principally Syderstone, and as an heiress she was a desirable bride for the highest in the land. In 1549 she met a very eligible young man. Kett's Rebellion had broken out and John Dudley, the Earl of Warwick, came up from London with an army to crush the rebels. Warwick's son, Robert Dudley, accompanied his father and met and fell in love with Amy. They married a year later and one of the wedding guests was the King of England, Edward VI, then about 12 years old. The couple lived in Norfolk and Robert became MP for the county. Then Edward VI died in 1553, bad news for the Dudley family who were Protestants. The heiress was Mary, Edward's much older sister, who was a Catholic.

The Dudleys led a rising to try to stop Mary getting the throne. They said that the next Queen of England should be Mary's cousin's daughter, Lady Jane Grey, who was married to one of the Dudley brothers. Robert Dudley proclaimed Lady Jane Grey Queen of England at King's Lynn, then one of the country's most important ports, but it all came to nothing. The Dudleys were imprisoned in the Tower, but Robert was luckier than most of the others as he was pardoned and released. Queen Mary died in 1558 and her half-sister Elizabeth came to the throne. She was a Protestant - and the Dudleys were back in favour. Robert and Elizabeth became very close friends and gossip at the court said they were lovers. There was also speculation about plans to marry and the chances of Robert becoming king. But there was one big snag ... Robert already had a wife, Amy.

She was sent to live in a country house in Oxfordshire, and on Sunday, September 8th 1560, all the servants were given leave to go to the fair. When they returned they found Amy's body at the foot of the great stairs in the hall, with her neck broken. Did she fall - or was she pushed?

The gossip said Robert Dudley had ordered a friend to throw Amy downstairs, so to break her neck and to place her body as if she had fallen. Amy's maid said she had heard her mistress "pray to God to deliver her from desperation". It is possible that Amy committed suicide. Her husband was entangled with another woman - and she was the Queen of England!.

Elizabeth did not marry Robert Dudley. She did not marry at all. That decision brought the House of Stuart to the English throne.

Was Amy Robsart's death an accident? Was it suicide? Could it have been murder? These questions have never been answered convincingly.

John Rolfe (1585-1622)

Celebrity wife

John Rolfe came from a well-known West Norfolk family who lived at Heacham Hall. He married in 1608 and his wife was pregnant when they boarded the *Sea Adventure,* part of a nine-ship fleet carrying colonists to Virginia. The ship was wrecked in a great storm, but from some of the timbers the crew managed to build two small pinnaces, and in these craft they eventually reached Virginia in May 1610.

They found the settlement in a state of strife and sickness, and relations with the local Indians were anything but harmonious. Over a period Rolfe became one of the leading men of the settlement, and became the first of them to successfully cultivate a marketable tobacco. His wife died and he remarried. The lady's name was Pocahontas, often described as an Indian princess. Certainly she was the daughter of the most important Indian chief in the area.

She evidently saved the life of a Captain John Smith in 1607. He hailed from Lincolnshire, but had King's Lynn connections. The Indians were going to kill him, but Pocahontas threw herself between him and his potential murderers. The tale has been embellished, but in 1616 John Rolfe and his new wife, now a Christian and renamed Rebecca, together with their child, came to England. She became a celebrity and was presented at court. Sadly, the English climate did not agree with her and she died in March 1617, on the eve of her departure back to America. Rolfe married again and returned to Virginia where he died.

From the son of Pocahontas have descended some of the most famous families in the United States, one descendant being the wife of President Wilson.

In the church at Heacham is a fine alabaster portrait of Pocahontas by a pupil of Rodin. It shows her in the English dress of her day, with a high hat and a fan of three feathers.

Walter Rye (1834-1929)

Norfolk books

Although he didn't move to Norfolk until he retired at 56 as a solicitor in London, Walter Rye left a bold mark on the county. His main memorial is his great collection of Norfolk books and manuscripts. It was a poor year in which he did not publish a couple of books.

Walter Rye was the last Mayor of Norwich in 1908-9 before the office was elevated in the following year to the dignity of a Lord Mayoralty. He detested formal dress and liked old clothes. During Rye's term of office King Edward VII, a stickler for etiquette on public occasions, paid the first visit by a reigning monarch to Norwich since 1671. To the utter dismay of all the other local bigwigs, Walter insisted on receiving the King in his customary tweeds.

From the age of 21 he spent all his holidays walking and cycling round Norfolk or sailing on the Broads. He noted on September 10th 1899: "I saw a beastly petrol launch for the first time on the Broads." He was an outstanding athlete, a champion walker, a good pistol shot and archer as well as a pioneer cyclist. He took to riding a tricycle in his old age.

Rye was one of the founders of the Broads Protection Society, and in 1891 fought and won a famous action to vindicate the public right of way across Hickling Broad. He restored St Leonard's Priory on the windy heights of Mousehold on the edge of Norwich. Buying and restoring old buildings became a very expensive hobby. He was for some years proprietor of the Maid's Head Hotel in Norwich, buying it to save it from being let to a brewer and kept it "to make people comfortable as I want to be myself."

He was fiercely proud that there was no older name in Norfolk at or after the Conquest than his own, and that the Barony of Rye of Hingham, had it not lapsed, would have been the oldest existent Norfolk peerage.

Frederick Savage (1828-1897)

Man of fair

Frederick Savage rose from poverty to wealth, earning his place as the showman's greatest benefactor on the way. An untutored mechanical genius, he thought up and constructed new amusements for the fair - and came very close to building the first motor cars in England.

Towards the end of his life, when his firm had achieved international fame, he was approached by American financiers with plans and patent rights for the manufacture of motor cars. But the Boer War put paid to the investment.

He is remembered mainly for his work on behalf of the showmen of Great Britain. Before the introduction of steam power, pleasure-riding devices were of a primitive character. When Savage harnessed steam to the roundabout he placed within the travelling showman's reach an invention which brought about the biggest changes in the fair world since the Middle Ages. Improvements did not end with the roundabouts themselves; the methods of illumination, decoration and music made marked progress. Then electricity led to further refinements.

He was born at Hevingham, near Aylsham, and at 16 found work in a foundry at East Dereham. He put enough money by to make a move to King's Lynn four years later. He made iron and wooden rakes, steam-powered drills and threshing machines. With investment from farmers, Savage was able to build a traction engine called the "Juggernaut", which crept along at three miles an hour, pulling threshing machines and ploughs, or delivering coal or manure.

His success was ensured when his machinery won praise at the Lynn Agricultural Show of 1864. The business was transferred to St Nicholas Street, where it received another boost from the construction of Alexandra Dock. Savage was employed to build hydraulic coal-drops and cranes for the dock company. He also turned his talents towards Lynn's February Mart, and the building of fairground roundabouts was an established part of the firm by the 1880s.

His inventions marked a new era in the history of the show world and he was honoured by engineering societies at home and abroad. He took a leading role in the civic life of Lynn and became Mayor in 1889. His term was a popular one, and at the end a statue to mark his outstanding career was subscribed to by his friends and erected near the old South Gates.

Clement Scott (1841-1904)

"Poppyland"

The writer who thought up the name "Poppyland", an area based mainly on and around the North Norfolk coast, Scott's articles in the Daily Telegraph, coupled with the opening of the railway to the district, helped make Cromer a fashionable resort.

He arrived in Cromer in August 1883, on the new railway line, but soon discovered a place more to his liking during a ramble along the cliff top. Sidestrand, with its crumbling cliffs and fields dotted with poppies, became the haven of peace he had been yearning for. His series of articles under the title "Poppyland - by a Holiday-  maker written at a farmhouse by the sea" caught the imagination of the public and also lured literary person- alities to the area. The eminent Victorian poet Algernon Charles Swinburne and his friend and fellow-writer Theodore Watts-Dunton led the way, and it became fashionable for London's literary and artistic society, and those who paid court to it, to make for "Poppyland".

Scott, as the man who discovered it, remained the doyen of its visitors, and he continued to make the journey there for 15 years, not only in the summer but also in midwinter. He wrote the famous poem "The Garden of Sleep" while standing in the churchyard by the old church tower at Christmas in 1885. It became a ritual for him to see in the New Year from the same spot, reading his poem as a reminder of the first days of his discovery and, in some ways, as a lament for what his publicity had done to the place.

He had his regrets by 1890 ... "The Cromer that we visit now is not the Cromer I wrote about a few years ago as my beloved Poppyland." He felt the area to be doomed, often wishing he had kept it to himself to prevent it from becoming "Bungalow Land". Scott later published "Blossom Land and Fallen Leaves" in which he expanded the story of "Poppyland" and rambled further afield in the Norfolk countryside. Before his first fateful visit to Norfolk, Scott was already a highly influential writer, especially in the field of dramatic criticism.

A water-trough monument, now filled with flowers, was placed on the Overstrand to Northrepps road in memory of the man who discovered "Poppyland".

Edward Seago (1910-1974)

Coronation artist

One of the country's most popular landscape artists this century, Edward Seago was born in Norwich, the son of a coal merchant. His work enjoyed great popularity during his lifetime, despite a lack of critical acclaim. He  developed a heart complaint as a child, but went on to ride, fly, sail, and even involve himself in pre-war espionage. Seago, who had a little art tuition from East Anglian artist Bertram Priestman, staged his first one-man London exhibition at 19 and the following year he had a painting selected for the Royal Academy.

A travelling circus and the world of ballet provided early inspiration for his work. He wrote nine books and collaborated on three volumes of verse and pictures with the Poet Laureate, John Masefield. On the outbreak of war, he concealed his heart trouble to enlist and became a camouflage officer.

In 1953, Seago became an official artist of the Coronation. He was a frequent visitor to Sandringham, and in 1956 he accompanied Prince Philip on *Britannia* on a trip to Antarctica, exhibiting the resulting paintings at St James' Palace.

Seago was always delighted to come back to East Anglia - his home was The Dutch House at Ludham - and he influenced many other local artists. He was equally at home in oils and watercolour. He was dogged by periods of disability throughout his life and a brain tumour killed him at 53. His ashes were scattered over the Norfolk marshes he had loved.

He painted portraits of many of the theatrical personalities who became his friends, including Noel Coward, Donald Sinden, Peter Cushing, Michael Dennison and Dulcie Gray. During the war, Seago became a friend and painting companion of his COs, General Auchinleck and General Alexander. When the latter was appointed Allied Commander in Chief in Italy he smuggled Seago out of England to be with him in the final stages of the campaign.

Derek and Hugh Seagrim

Hero brothers

The Seagrims, their exploits marked on the village sign in their home parish of Whissonsett, are the only brothers to win the country's top two awards for bravery. Lt Col Derek Seagrim took command of the 7th Battalion Green Howards for the Western Desert campaign in the last war. During the offensive at the Mareth Line he accounted for 20 of the enemy, totally disregarding his own safety and setting an outstanding example to his own men. However, he died of his wounds and in May 1943, the posthumous award of the

Victoria Cross was announced. His mother, Mrs Amelia Seagrim, went to Buckingham Palace to receive the decoration from the King. Three years later, Mrs Seagrim made history when she again went to the Palace to receive a posthumous award. This time it was the George Cross awarded to Major Hugh Seagrim in recognition of his work and self-sacrifice in Burma. He loved the Karen people and it was to save them from brutal persecution from the Japanese that he surrendered in 1944. After enduring long periods of solitary confinement, he was executed by the Japanese.

Anna Sewell (1820-1878)

Horse's tale

A year before she died Anna Sewell produced her only book, "Black Beauty". This autobiography of a horse became one of the world's best sellers with over 30 million copies sold. It was written in the White House at Old Catton on the outskirts of Norwich and had a big influence on the general treatment and care of horses.

Born in Great Yarmouth, Anna inherited her mother's gift for writing. Confined to the house by an injury which crippled her in her teens, Anna developed her writing along with a deep feeling for animals. Although the family moved from Yarmouth to London when Anna was two, she spent many childhood summers on her grandfather's farm at Buxton in Norfolk. She died six years before her mother, never knowing the success "Black Beauty" was about to achieve, and she and her parents were buried in the Quaker burial ground at Lamas, near Coltishall.

"Black Beauty" was originally intended not for children but for the working folk of Victorian times ... those in daily contact with horses. A note at the back of all early editions recommended further reading for "those who wish to know more of the right treatment of horses on the road and in the stable".

It wasn't until she was 60 that Mary Sewell, Anna's mother, began to write. One of her stories "Mother's Last Words", sold over a million copies. Anna and her brother, Philip, were both taught at home by their strong-willed mother.

In the north-east corner of Yarmouth market place, nestling in the shadow of the parish church, stands the house where Anna was born. It has been used as a restaurant and tea-room in recent years, although there are plenty of indications that the building owes its high profile after restoration to the woman who wrote "Black Beauty".

The Sewell Barn Theatre is next to the Blyth-Jex School in Norwich. Philip Sewell owned a farm on the site, and a barn, the last remaining building, was converted into a theatre and opened in 1979. Tradition has it that the horse which inspired "Black Beauty" was stabled in the barn.

Thomas Shadwell (1642-1692)

Poet from Weeting

Shadwell was a poet and dramatist born in Weeting and educated at Cambridge. He became Poet Laureate in 1668 after Dryden, with whom he had a long-standing feud in print. Shadwell produced a version of a Moliere play "The Suillen Lovers" at Lincoln's Inn Fields, and other works include an opera "The Enchanted Island", adapted from Shakespeare's "The Tempest". His plays "Epsom Wells" and "Bury Fair" give an interesting glimpse of contemporary life, manners and amusements.

Cloudesley Shovell (1650-1707)

"The other Nelson"

Often described as "Norfolk's other Nelson", Cloudesley Shovell was born in Cockthorpe, went to sea at 14 and took the legendary ladder from cabin boy to admiral. His early rise in the Navy coincided with William of Orange's ascent to the English throne. Shovell distinguished himself at the Battle of Bantry Bay - for which he was knighted - and went on to a series of victories ... La Hogue, Gibraltar, Barcelona and Beachy Head.

By now a rear-admiral, Shovell and his commander Lord Torrington faced a French armada of 100 vessels with just 56 ships off the Sussex coast. With Louis XIV's army victorious in Flanders, London swarming with Jacobites and William campaigning in Ulster, the fate of England was in the balance. Had the French affected a landing the country must have fallen - but after sorting out the allied fleet in the Channel, they failed to finish off the survivors bottled up in the Thames. Excessive caution saved England.

Torrington's own caution met with the fury of his monarch and a period of confinement in the Tower. Shovell, his courage a source of pride and consolation, went on to distinguish himself above all in the War of Spanish Succession, which established Britain as a great power.

Returning to England after the siege of Toulon, the English fleet, through a navigational error, sailed onto the rocks of the Isles of Scilly. Several ships, including Shovell's *Association,* were wrecked. One story goes that Shovell survived and was found in a semi-conscious state by a woman prowling the beach. She is said to have killed England's naval hero after spotting an emerald ring, confessing to her crime 30 years later on her death bed.

Sir Cloudesley was buried in Westminster Abbey. A monument in the second bay of the south aisle of the nave has been described as "an extraordinary pompous celebration". It consists of a sarcophagus on which reclines the figure of a man in Roman armour. The base is made up of panels carved with various trophies and a shipwreck. It is flanked with Corinthian columns which support entablatures and cherubs.

John Skelton (1460-1529)

Poet joker

Generally considered to be the first poet laureate, John Skelton was Rector of Diss for 25 years, from 1504 until his death. Before moving to Norfolk he had been tutor to Prince Henry - later Henry VIII - and claimed to have taught the prince to spell. (Presumably Henry taught himself to count when wives started to appear on the scene!).

Although he was a fine scholar, Skelton was also by character a scurrilous and vituperative rebel who took considerable delight in the crudeness of medieval life. This expressed itself most forcibly in his poetry which he used as a deadly weapon to attack his enemies. As he became a legendary figure a collection of stories about him was published - "The Merrie Tales of Maister Skelton, very pleasant for the  recreation of the minde." Many are extremely coarse and none of them wholly authentic.

One of the most famous yarns concerns his keeping a concubine at Diss, by whom he had several children. His parishioners complained and he was summoned to the Bishop's Palace in Norwich. He took with him two chickens as a gift. The Bishop was very angry from the first moment of their meeting. Skelton became just as enraged. Although he castigated him severely, the Bishop was still willing to accept Skelton's gift. The Rector of Diss said: "My Lord, my capons have proper names. This capon is named Alpha - this is the first capon that I did ever give to you. And this capon is named Omega ... and this is the last capon that ever I will give to you and so fare you well."

A joke which misfired was Skelton's attack in verse on Cardinal Wolsey for his luxurious lifestyle. It is thought Wolsey twice put him in prison. On his death-bed Skelton is said to have claimed he was married to his concubine, but had confessed to adultery (only a venial sin) rather than to marriage, at that time a capital crime for a priest. He is buried in Westminster Abbey.

He was an acid-penned satirist, but also wrote poetry of great originality and lasting worth ... "Philip Sparrow", for example, the lament of a small girl for her pet sparrow.

George Skipper (1856-1948)

Exotic buildings

An architect famed for the originality and sheer exuberance of his buildings, George Skipper was born in East Dereham, the son of a building contractor. He made the Cromer skyline erupt with the turrets and towers and exotic extravagance of his hotels. He brought a touch of the Arabian Nights to the centre of Norwich with his Royal Arcade.

Nickolaus Pevsner described it as "innocent in front, but very naughty once its back is turned." Joseph Stannard designed the "innocent" front; Skipper was responsible for all the "naughtiness". He astonished Lowestoft with

a white stuccoed, wide-windowed yacht club. He designed major buildings in London and other parts of the country, but it is in Suffolk, Cambridgeshire and most especially in Norfolk that he left the largest imprint of his unmistakable flamboyance - from the private Victorian villas in city and county to the grandeur of works like the Norwich Union Life Office with its superb marble hall and boardroom, the Telephone Area Office in St Giles and Sennowe Park at Guist.

As a boy, George Skipper wanted to be an artist, and it was only because of his father's wishes that he joined an architect's office in London. He qualified at 23 and set up his own practice a year later in Norwich. In 1889 he was commissioned to design a new town hall for Cromer. Until then his designs were fairly straightforward, but in the next few years he worked on a succession of increasingly enriched and romantic hotels culminating in the Hotel de Paris, a picturesque extravaganza rising above the promenade.

He was established from then on. His daring and acclaim increased and he explored all sorts of style possibilities from the French Renaissance and Art Nouveau to the Italian Baroque.

George Skipper's son Edward continued the architectural trend and qualified to continue the practice when his father died at the age of 94. Several design awards followed to keep the family name to the fore.

James Edward Smith (1759-1828)

Leading Botanist

James Smith, born in Norwich, was a distinguished medical man and botanist who bought the botanical collection of the Swede Carl Linnaeus for £1000 and formed the Linnaean Society. He was knighted for his services to the science of botany, and was also a leading nonconformist of his time. In 1818 Sir James became a candidate for the chair of botany at Cambridge, but not being a member of the Church of England, he was not considered eligible by the university authorities.

Frank Stone (1909-1988)

"Mr Yarmouth"

A leading figure in the public, political, trade union and civic life of Great Yarmouth through several decades, Frank Stone died a few months short of achieving the remarkable feat of serving on the borough council for 50 successive years. The man who became known as "Mr Yarmouth" through his long and varied service to the town had been given the chance to aim for that golden jubilee when the Conservatives did not put up a candidate against him in his ward.

That was a measure of the esteem in which he was held by supporters and opponents alike. He was twice Mayor of Yarmouth, in 1947 and 1966, a Freeman of the borough (1969) "for eminent, valuable and distinguished services", life member of the Trade Union Congress after a record 43 years as chairman of the local trades council, chairman of Norfolk County Council (1975 - 6) and a deputy lieutenant of the county. His feat of 49 years of unbroken service was on Yarmouth Town Council and the borough council that succeeded it with local government reorganisation in 1974.

A notable family record was established when Mr Stone, his wife Mildred (after whom the council named an old people's home) and their son, Frank junior, were all on the council together.

His active involvement began as a 13-year-old Cobholm lad, delivering handbills for the Labour candidate for Yarmouth in the 1918 General Election. His working life was as a shipwright at Fellows' Southtown yard and for years he was chairman of the local branch of the associated trade union. He won a seat on the old town council at the fourth attempt in 1938. He served continuously until his death nearly half a century later. In 1959 Frank Stone tried to widen his political horizons

by standing as a Parliamentary candidate for Central Norfolk in the General Election, but he was unsuccessful. He continued in numerous local posts, and for years led the Labour group on the council. When he died in June, 1988, Yarmouth's Conservative MP, Michael Cartiss, praised him as a man whose commitment to the town was "unrivalled".

John Stubbs (died 1591)

Loyal subject

Stubbs lived at Thelveton near Diss. He died in 1591, and is cited by historians as proof that her subjects loved Queen Elizabeth I with the sort of deep affection no other sovereign ever won. Stubbs was arrested for publishing a protest against the proposed marriage of the Queen with a Roman Catholic. He was found guilty and sentenced to have his right hand cut off, the punishment to be carried out on a scaffold put up at Westminster. Stubbs, awaiting his fate, declared to the crowd that he was warmly attached to the Queen and the punishment would in no way impair his loyalty. After his hand had been cut off, he removed his hat with his left hand and cried: "God save the Queen!".

Richard Taverner

Translated Bible

Taverner, who translated the Bible and printed his own version of it in 1545, was brought up at Brisley, a few miles from East Dereham, before he went on to shine as a scholar at Oxford and Cambridge. He lies at Wood Easton in Oxfordshire, but his father John was buried at Brisley, his brass shield marking his grave in the nave.

"Turnip" Townshend (1674-1738)

Statesman and farmer

Charles Townshend inherited the Raynham estate in Norfolk and the title of second Viscount in 1687. He was a champion of progressive farming, earning his nickname from the root crop he introduced with such enthusiasm. His turnips meant that cattle, instead of being slaughtered in October, could be fed in the stall and that sheep could be folded on the land.

The Norfolk four-course system favoured by Townshend gave a rotation of wheat, roots and grasses sown among barley for the ensuing year. The years between his retirement from politics in 1730 and his death in 1738 were spent almost entirely at Raynham.

Born with all the advantages needed to enter political life he spent almost two decades in high office, directing  Britain's foreign policy through the changeover from the Stuart to the Hanoverian period. He married a sister of Sir Robert Walpole, and is known not only for the honourable role he played in European politics but also for his unsullied integrity. Lord Chesterfield wrote of him that "never minister had cleaner hands". He led the first government of George I as Secretary of State, only to become second fiddle to Walpole in 1721 after the bursting of the South Sea Bubble.

Nine years later Walpole succeeded in driving Townshend out of office. He retired to his country seat at Raynham to follow the agricultural pursuits that made him famous as "Turnip" Tonwshend. He was encouraging innovations in farming methods a generation before the more publicised developments of the "agricultural revolution". Even before his death his reputation as an improving landowner was well established through the granting of long leases with detailed husbandry clauses.

When in 1776 Coke inherited his estate at Holkham to become another famous leader in agricultural developments, he was able to follow Townshend's inspired Norfolk footsteps.

George Vancouver (1757-1798)

Key explorer

Born in King's Lynn, George Vancouver now stands proudly among the most select band of explorer-navigators. He commemorated his family and many of the places connected with them in the names he gave to areas he discovered and explored.

The map of the coast of north-west Canada is dotted with names carrying Norfolk connections. There's a Lynn Channel, a Holkham Bay, a Port Snettisham and a Port Houghton. There's a Port Coke (after Thomas Coke) and a Port Windham (after the Norfolk statesman William Windham)

Vancouver sailed as a boy with Captain Cook and years later, in following the course of Cook, he rounded the Cape and surveyed the south-west coast of Australia, naming harbours and headlands. He sailed round the west coast of North America exploring tiny inlets and discovering the Gulf of Georgia, and then sailed round the island which now bears his name. Bred to rigid discipline at sea he was  himself a strict disciplinarian and there was an outcry when he flogged a midshipman, put him in irons and discharged him from the ship.

Vancouver returned home in 1795 with his health destroyed. He died three years later with the editing of his journals unfinished. The work was completed by his brother John and published under the title "A Voyage of Discovery to the North Pacific Ocean and Round the World" - a fitting memorial to the most able of Cook's "young gentlemen".

Earlier this century it was written, "Vancouver is undoubtedly the worst documented of all the famous 18th century navigators. He did his work. He died. He was forgotten." That is no longer the case, although he seems to be remembered more in Canada, where a statue of him sits atop the Parliament Building in Victoria.

Matthew Vassar (1792-1868)

College founder

Destined to become a successful brewer, and to achieve fame as the founder of a great college in America, Matthew Vassar was born in East Tuddenham, a few miles from East Dereham. He was only four when the family went across the Atlantic.

His father bought a farm, grew barley and made home-brewed beer. The Vassar brewery was started in 1801,

 but disaster overtook the family ten years later. The brewery was burnt down, and on the following day Matthew's elder brother was killed while descending into a vat charged with carbonic acid gas. Matthew went into business on his own, opening an oyster saloon in connection with a brewery. After 20 years of highly successful business he was able to build a large new brewery on the Hudson.

He was 54 - but his most important work had yet to begin. On a visit to London with his wife in 1845 he visited Guy's Hospital, which had been founded by a friend of his, Thomas Guy. Vassar was so impressed by the good work being done at Guy's he began to consider the possibility of using his fortune for some similar benefaction. He returned to America and conceived and developed his plan of building and endowing a college for young women which should be to them "what Yale and Harvard are to young men".

So started Vassar College, near Poughkeepsie in New York State, the dream of a Norfolk man who became a pioneer of women's education in the United States. He founded the college in 1861, but the Civil War delayed the formal opening until 1865.

Doreen Wallace (1897-1989)

Tithe war

Campaigner, writer and artist Doreen Rash - who wrote over 50 books under the pen-name of Doreen Wallace - gained national recognition in a 40-year battle to abolish what she described as "the iniquitous tithe tax".

A former landowner and farmer in Wortham, near Diss, she became president of the National Tithe Payers' Association before the last war. In 1934 she and her husband barricaded their farm during a six-week siege after her refusal to pay the Church of England tithe. Eventually 134 pigs and 15 cattle worth £700 were seized in lieu of the tax and a memorial recording the event was erected.

In the summer of 1939 she decided to see if the church really would make a person bankrupt - so she refused to pay again. This time her furniture and bedding were taken from the house and auctioned. But the auctioneer was a close friend and the furniture was bought by other members of the association. The payment, traditionally one-tenth of a landowner's profits, had to be paid to the church and was later collected by the Inland Revenue. It was abolished in 1967.

On her death at 92, the Eastern Daily Press called her a latter-day Boadicea: "Here was no ordinary lady of the manor. Doreen Wallace remained a trenchant East Anglian non-conformist of the secular kind almost up to the end of her life". She died at her Diss home.

In 1951, she joined forces with naturalist Dick Bagnall-Oakeley to produce "Norfolk" in the County Books series. She was deeply concerned about the changing face of local life, and in a typically forthright article in the EDP in February 1986 she sized up the village picture: "There are people in villages who have never spoken together, who are not known to the real villagers either by sight or by name ... the most useless 'foreigners' are those whose country retreat is only meant for weekend and summer breaks. They don't even arrive unless the weather invites. They can never become part of country life."

Saint Walstan (961-1016)

Holy and humble

Norfolk's patron saint of agriculture was born in Bawburgh, a few miles from Norwich, the son of Benedict and Blide (or Blida) herself venerated as a saint and buried in her own chapel at Martham near Great Yarmouth.

At the age of 12 Walstan decided to leave the security of his home, give up his inheritance and live the simple life of a worker on the land. He walked to Taverham where  a farmer offered shelter and work. Poverty, humility and charity became his life as he gave away all he had to the poor and needy.

He had a premonition of his death and said he wanted his body to be put in a farm cart drawn by two oxen, and he was to be buried wherever they stopped. The oxen stopped at Bawburgh Church. Bishop Algar of Elmham took the burial service and such was the reputation of this holy and humble man that the Bishop there and then declared Walstan to be a saint.

So on May 30th, 1016, began a story which is now legend. The waters of Saint Walstan's Well at Bawburgh became renowned for their curative properties for humans and animals alike. The Walstan legend spread to several other Norfolk parishes and even further afield. His image is found on rood screens, panels and in stained glass.

Variations on the familiar figure, scythe in hand and with a variety of animals at his feet, can be seen at Sparham, Barnham Broome, Burlingham St Andrew and Litcham. The Catholic church at Costessey is dedicated to him. At Ludham he has one of the 12 painted panels of the rood screen, and there is a stained glass window in his name in St Thomas' Church in Norwich.

The most recent dedication took place in 1989 when a memorial and cell were dedicated to Saint Walstan in Bowthorpe, on the outskirts of Norwich, by the Rt Rev David Bentley, Bishop of Lynn. The parish church of SS Mary and Walstan at Bawburgh is still a centre for pilgrimage. Each year a procession is made from the church to the famous well and a service of blessing performed.

Robert Walpole (1676-1745)

Rests in Norfolk

Walpole, the first statesman to be recognised as Britain's Prime Minister, took 13 years to build Houghton Hall, the biggest country house in Norfolk. It was completed in 1735. Sir Robert, who died in 1745, lies in the family vault in the little church nearby. He held the office of Prime Minister longer than anyone else, 21 years of uninterrupted control of the government. He built the tower at Houghton and the porch of the church which shelters him.

John Wesley (1703-1791)

A Regular visitor

John Wesley, the founder of Methodism, was a regular visitor to Norfolk when roads were rough and horses had to be sturdy. Norwich, Great Yarmouth and King's Lynn were his three strategic centres and he didn't spare the blushes when it came to saying what he thought of them. In the Tabernacle in Norwich he told his audience they were "the most ignorant, conceited, self-willed, fickle, intractable, disorderly, disjointed society in the three kingdoms." Yarmouth fared little better .. "a large and populous town and as eminent for wickedness and ignorance as any resort in England." Lynn picked up garlands all the way with the people "affable and humane, open and frank, good-natured and courteous." He must have been asked back for tea at a thousand homes after that 1771 eulogy.

Jimmy "Paris" West (1896-1987)

Famous rescue

"Paris" West was the last surviving member of the crew of the old rowing and sailing lifeboat, the *J C Madge*, which accomplished the most famous sea rescue in Sheringham's lifeboat history. It was in 1916 when the *Ulla*, laden with coal and bound for the Thames, struck a sandbank and drifted helplessly in appalling conditions. The lifeboat, at sea for more than 48 hours, rescued the crew of 23. "Paris", a member of one of the town's oldest-established fishing families, died at the age of 91 in 1987.

Henry Williamson (1897-1977)

Norfolk farm

The dreamer came face to face with reality in 1937 when Henry Williamson stopped writing romantic novels about Devon - and became a Norfolk farmer. Drained of inspiration after writing 20 books of wildlife and countryside fantasy, including the classics "Tarka the Otter" and "Salar the Salmon", he invested his entire capital in a small, run-down farm at Stiffkey in North Norfolk.

He had scarcely any idea about farming and the adventures are told, not without humour, in "The Story Of A Norfolk Farm", first published in 1941 and dedicated "to all who have worked and suffered for the land and the people of Great Britain".

Williamson had explored Norfolk on a bicycle in 1912, but the later decision to move east came after a chance meeting with his publisher and friend Dick De La Mare, son of the poet, who already had a country home in Norfolk. Eventually Williamson became disenchanted with some local people who spread rumours about him being in league with Germany, and suggested that even the skylights in his studio were arranged in such a way so as to signal to Luftwaffe navigators. He returned to Devon and wrote 17 more books.

"As I look back on the past two years, I am glad they will not come again" wrote Williamson. "For one period, of about three months, I thought I would not be able to keep on. During those months I worked on the farm by day, taught myself the building trade, drove the tractor, was continually striving to give others a new outlook, and often wrote until one or two o'clock in the morning".

During his time in Norfolk, Williamson befriended local writer Lilias Rider Haggard. He noticed her column in the Eastern Daily Press celebrating the East Anglian countryside, and persuaded her to let him edit the diaries. The resulting book, "Norfolk Life", first published in 1943, remains a firm favourite.

Angus Wilson (died 1991)

Writing course

Angus Wilson, a founder member of the University of East Anglia and a major influence on younger writers, died at 77 in May 1991. One of Britain's foremost literary figures, he began teaching at the UEA in 1963, later becoming a professor, and helped set up a creative writing course with which such authors as Ian McEwan, Rose Tremain and Booker Prize winner Kazuo Ishiguro were associated. Knighted in 1980, Sir Angus wrote about 50 books. A special dinner was held in his honour in 1989 as part of the university's 25th anniversary celebrations.

Arthur Knyvet Wilson (1842-1921)

Victoria Cross

One of the few Royal Navy officers to win the Victoria Cross, Arthur Knyvet Wilson was born in Swaffham, where his grandfather was vicar for 65 years. He won his VC on February 29th, 1884, at El Teb while he was captain of *HMS Hecla*, and he was presented with a sword by the officers of the torpedo school to mark his achievement.

On his return home to Swaffham he was greeted at the railway station by a vast crowd and the shops were closed for the occasion. A strict disciplinarian, he was known as "Old 'ard 'eart" to his sailors, but they still held him in great respect. He was responsible for several inventions and innovations during a time when steam-driven ironclads were taking over from wooden hulled sailing ships. Sir Arthur first served on the *Victory*, rose

through the ranks and was an admiral when due to retire in 1907. However, a special Order in Council gave him five more years in service.

He spent two years of retirement in Swaffham and was then offered the post of First Sea Lord in succession to Lord Fisher. He retired once more to his home town, but in 1915 Winston Churchill called on him to help lead the Navy through the Great War. Retiring yet again in 1918, Sir Arthur became involved in local works, helping to design Swaffham golf course and the town war memorial. He is buried in Swaffham churchyard, and a memorial plaque and a copy of his Victoria Cross citation are in the church. Sir Arthur Knyvet Wilson Bt. VC, GCB, OM, GCVO, DCL - ranking alongside Norfolk's greatest naval figures. The VC citation reads:

"On the 29th February, 1884, at the battle of El Teb, Sudan, Captain Wilson of the HMS Hecla, attached himself during the advance to the right-half battery, Naval Brigade, in place of a lieutenant who was mortally wounded. As the troops closed on the enemy battery, the Arabs charged out on the detachment which was dragging one of the guns, whereupon Captain Wilson sprang to the front and engaged in single combat with some of the enemy, and so protected the detachment until men of the York and Lancaster Regiment came to his assistance."

Saint Withburga (died 654)

Healing water

The legend of Saint Withburga is depicted in the East Dereham town sign which spans the High Street at its junction with the market place. Anna, King of the East Angles, was killed at the Battle of Blythburgh by the heathen King Penda. Withburga, youngest of Anna's four daughters, vowed to become a nun and settled in a village which later became known as Dereham.

She set out to build a church but food was scarce and she prayed for help. The story goes that the Virgin Mary appeared to Withburga telling her to go to a nearby stream - possibly Washbridge - where every day two does would stand to be milked. When the town bailiff found out he vowed to kill the deer, but his horse stumbled at a fence and he broke his neck when he was thrown.

Withburga was buried in Dereham Churchyard. Dereham and Ely were always closely connected. The Abbot of Ely was the owner of the manor of East Dereham, and Ely had been founded by Withburga's sister Ethelreda. The Abbot decided to steal Withburga's body, and in 974 he and his monks removed it to Ely Cathedral where it was interred near her royal sisters, Saint Ethelreda and Saint Saxburga. It was said not to have decomposed, and after her body was stolen a spring said to have healing qualities issued from her tomb.

The Ancient Guild of Saint Withburga was revived in Dereham in 1990. The guild was first established in 975. In the Middle Ages there were 15 guilds in Dereham and the Guildhall was the centre of the Guild of Saint Withburga.

The Dereham town sign was put up in 1954 on the 1300th anniversary of the death of Withburga. It was carved by Harry Carter of Swaffham and presented to the town by the local Rotary Club.

James Woodforde (1740-1803)

Parson's diary

First published between 1924 and 1931, the five-volume diary of Parson James Woodforde places him alongside Kilvert, Evelyn and Pepys. Born in Somerset and educated at New College, Oxford, he held a number of curacies before being appointed in 1774 to the living of Weston Longville, a few miles from Norwich.

His diary, kept from the age of 18 until a few weeks before his death, is a mine of information about the lives of ordinary people in the second half of the the 18th century - farmers, shopkeepers, servants, squires, clergy, doctors, blacksmiths and merchants.

While great events such as the emergence of America and the French Revolution were being enacted in the

wider world, Woodforde's diary records the thoughts and deeds of the parson as he busied himself with the concerns of village life.

A sociable bachelor he was looked after by his niece Nancy and five servants, and constantly showed a reverence for small events and the domestic odds and ends of existence. The diary is also a meticulously kept account book, with the price of food, stage-coaches, household necessities, theatres and medicines all carefully entered.

There are many amusing interludes with this entry a strong favourite:

April 15,1778: Brewed a vessel of strong Beer today. My two large Piggs, by drinking some Beer grounds taking out of one of my Barrels today, got so amazingly drunk by it, that they were not able to stand and appeared like dead things almost, and so remained all night from dinner time today. I never saw Piggs so drunk in my life. I slit their ears for them without feeling.

April 16: My 2 Piggs are still unable to walk yet, but they are better than they were yesterday. They tumble about the yard and can by no means stand at all steady yet. In the afternoon my 2 Piggs were tolerably sober.

The weather demanded close attention throughout the diary:

January 28, 1794 Two women froze to death Saturday last going from Norwich Market to their home.

January 21, 1795: The last Night, the most severest yet, extreme cold. So cold that the Poultry kept in the Cart-Shed and obliged to be driven out to be fed.

Richard Woodget (1847-1928)

Cutty Sark

Woodget, born at Burnham Norton, became the most famous captain of the clipper ship, The *Cutty Sark*. Captain Woodget joined the clipper in 1885 and kept the job for ten years. He drove his ship and his crews hard, regularly making the voyage out to Australia in 70 days and coming back in 80. Men who trained under him usually had no problem in finding good jobs in their later careers, and many rose to the top of their profession. For many years on his retirement Captain Woodget was local collector for the Shipwrecked Fishermen and Mariners Royal Benevolent Society. That institution subscribed for the stone anchor on his grave at Burnham Norton.

Photographic credits: Most photographs are from the authors own collections. Thanks are also extended to John Baxter, David Butters, Commander Mark Cheyne, Miss Lorna Clarke, Terry Davy Collection, Dereham Antiquarian Society, Eastern Counties Newspaper, Noel Edward, Alan Howard, Norfolk Naturalists' Trust, Norwich Union, Sir Julian Paget, Royal National Lifeboat Institution, Edward Skipper, Beryl Tooley, The Marquess Townshend, and Carol Twinch.

Richard 'Dick' Condon (1937-1991)

The Norfolk connection at work .... Keith Skipper with Dick Condon, the man who turned Norwich's Theatre Royal into one of the most successful theatres in Europe after taking over as general manager in 1972. Mr Condon died in his native Ireland at the age of 54 just as this book was going to print.